Good Times, Good Grilling

CHERYL AND BILL JAMISON

Good Times, Good Grilling

Surefire Recipes for Great Grill Parties

WILLIAM MORROW

An Imprint of HarperCollinsPublishers

To the newest party girl in our family,
granddaughter Chloe Brooklyn Neale,
a charmer from the beginning

HarperCollins books may be purchased for educational, business, or sales promotional use. For information, please write: Special Markets Department, HarperCollins Publishers Inc., 10 East 53rd Street,.New York, NY 10022.

FIRST EDITION

Printed on acid-free paper

Library of Congress Cataloging-in-Publication Data

Jamison, Cheryl Alters.
    Good times, good grilling: surefire recipes for great grill parties/
Cheryl and Bill Jamison.—1st ed.
        p.   cm.
    ISBN 0-06-053487-7
    1. Barbecue cookery.   2. Entertaining.   I. Jamison, Bill.   II. Title.
TX840.B3J355   2006
641.7'6—dc22   2004053072

05   06   07   08   09 ❖/TP 10   9   8   7   6   5   4   3   2   1

CONTENTS

ACKNOWLEDGMENTS

Almost every day is a party when you've got good friends. We count several colleagues among our best friends, especially literary agent Doe Coover, editor Harriet Bell, and their savvy support staffs. Deborah Durham, a.k.a. "the Goddess of Galisteo," also deserves special recognition for her invaluable business assistance.

Our old pal David Fraher will be surprised to see his name turn up in the chapter on "Spontaneous Combustion," but he did shape the nature of this book by sharing with us his approach to entertaining years ago. Donna Myers, who counsels and promotes the Hearth, Patio, and Barbecue Association, and is the only person in the world with more grills than us, can always be counted on for solid advice.

We learn new tricks regularly from our local grilling buddies, including Rob and Mary Coffland, Dave and Susan Curtis, Gayther and Susie Gonzalez, Ed and Ellen Reid, Bob and Nancy Schwan, Jim and Cindy Turner, and "Bumble Bee" Bob and BJ Weil. Whether they are joining us at our home, letting us make a mess in their outdoor kitchens, or cooking for us when we need a break, they are treasured friends.

Our thanks to these accomplices, and also to you, a valued reader who gives us the opportunity for all of this grilling, writing, and fun.

Spontaneous Combustion

Cooking for friends should always be fun, but too often even a small, casual party becomes complicated or intimidating. Inexperienced cooks and hosts naturally feel some anxiety, and that may be ratcheted up by the advice coming from professionals. Every television show on entertaining, every article on the subject in a magazine or newspaper, suggests that we should fret about what we serve, the table we set, the theme we address for the occasion. We must, we're told, contemplate, coordinate, decorate, create, and then officiate.

Nonsense. It's about friendship, and the sharing of good food and good times—nothing else.

This book shows how to make it easy and fail-proof, without serious planning, hassles, or time commitments. We'll grill for our friends, because it's a casual and lively way to entertain, and we'll detail how to grill the food to perfection every time. Our focus is on simple but flavorful dishes that even beginners can master, including variations that suggest ways to add signature touches of your own to wow your guests. We don't offer complex scenarios, or trendy tips, or instructions for folding napkins. Everything is about having fun with friends in a relaxed, fulfilling way.

THE KEY TO SUCCESS

It doesn't really matter whether you have matching silverware, a vase of flowers, a seating plan, or a freshly mowed lawn. What you do need for a successful grill party is hearty, satisfying food, the kind of fare that makes people feel special and indulged. Food should be the centerpiece of the event, not just a weak excuse for getting together. You want to stimulate appetites and spirits alike.

Forget fancy at this kind of party. It's much more important that you fixed the food and that the food fits you. If you're a pizza person, grill pizzas for your friends. Make them yourself and make them exceptional, with all the right flourishes for you and your guests. You'll feel like a star and they'll treat you like one.

We've carefully chosen the food in this book to reflect broad and strong interests. We deliberately avoid an encyclopedic approach, focusing instead on real favorites that you'll enjoy cooking again and again, and will feel proud to serve your friends. The concentration on a manageable range of dishes allows us to cover them thoroughly and allows you to learn them well.

Any cook, however inexperienced, can succeed admirably with any of the dishes. Start with the next chapter on "Grilling Basics," which describes general principles of professional-quality grilling that apply to all foods. Even if you've grilled for decades, the advice will help you refine your approach or reinforce your instincts. The recipe chapters provide specific grilling tips for the individual dishes, a critical consideration because you have to grill different foods in different ways for the best results.

ADOPTING SPECIALTIES

Many cooks will want to try a wide range of the recipes. If you're a novice or only an occasional cook, however, we suggest the approach we learned from David Fraher, a friend in Minneapolis. When we were on an extended road trip about ten years ago, the map indicated that Minneapolis was slightly less than a day's detour, so we called David to see whether we could get together if we made a brief stop in the city. He invited us to his place for an impromptu grill party, promising us one of his "specialties," which turned out to be terrific lamb burgers served with a seasonal salad.

When we raved about the dinner and his spur-of-the-moment hospitality, David chuckled and coyly confessed his secret about cooking for friends. "I only know how to cook three dishes," he said. "I have them down so well now that they're dead simple. I can make them at a moment's notice with no more hassle than a quick run to the grocery store."

Some people may prefer just one specialty, and others may opt for five, but the essence of the idea remains the same. You're always ready to grill for friends if you've mastered a select number of simple party dishes tailored to your own personal tastes. You can turn a neighborly conversation over the back fence into a spontaneous grill-out, invite coworkers home to celebrate an office coup, or entertain in-laws who drop by unexpectedly. You know what to grill and how to grill it before you even extend an invitation, so you're prepared to party at will.

In selecting possible specialties, bear in mind the capabilities of your grill. Good food options for you may be limited by the size of your cooking grate or the intensity of heat that your grill generates. The grilling instructions that accompany all the main dishes specify the appropriate heat levels for cooking. If the grate is small, shrimp is a better choice than pizza. If you cook on a gas grill that doesn't have real searing power, chicken will come out better than pork tenderloins. If you have an infrared grill that tends to stay hot, you're always on the verge of burning vegetables but skirt steak works great.

Try out a number of the dishes that appeal to you, making sure they excel on your type of grill. Pick your favorites among them and then tweak them with signature accents, using the suggested variations to stimulate your imagination. With a little practice, you'll be serving your specialties to friends for years to come.

Whether you take the specialty approach, or you're an accomplished cook prepared to grill any of our dishes, you've always got good food at the tip of your tongs. Add friends and stir gently. It's not the kind of spontaneous combustion you learned about in chemistry class, but it's a lot more fun for everyone, including you as the cook and host.

Grilling Basics

The most critical success factor in grilling has nothing to do with whether you cook with charcoal or gas, marinate your food in advance, or serve your meat with a special barbecue sauce. What counts the most is an understanding and appreciation of true grill flavor. That alone can qualify someone as a master griller, regardless of the state of their grill or their skills as a saucier. If you don't have that understanding, you can't even be sure you're really grilling when you cook on a grill.

All methods of cooking, from simmering to frying, produce distinctive tastes and textures. The goal in grilling is to intensify the natural flavor of food through the chemical process of high-heat browning (known in scientific circles as the Maillard reaction). With meat, fish, and poultry, the browning and crisping of the exterior requires direct heat at a relatively high temperature. The fire must be hot enough to shrink the muscle fibers on the surface, which concentrates the flavor, but not so hot that it burns or chars the outside before adequately cooking the inside. When you get it right, the result is a robust amplification of the food's natural flavor along with a scrumptious textural contrast between the crusted surface and the succulent interior. It's an outcome characteristic of grilling, unlike anything obtained by any other cooking method except open-flame rotisserie roasting. You may want to add other complementary seasonings to the food with spice rubs, marinades, sauces, or relishes, but they should never distract from the distinctive grill taste.

The only way to get that special flavor is to fully cook all surfaces of meat, fish, and poultry over direct heat. That's not difficult to do, but it isn't how many Americans grill at home. To cook entirely with direct heat requires keeping the grill open rather than covered, just as chefs do in restaurant kitchens. When you cook covered, as many American grill manufacturers recommend, you create an oven effect and do much of the cooking with the heat reflected off the lid. In effect, you are grilling and baking at the same time. The resulting flavor reflects the methodology, providing only a modicum of grilled texture along with a generic baked taste.

Using a cover simplifies the cooking process, particularly for inexperienced cooks, which is one of the main reasons manufacturers suggest it. You put the food in and leave it until it's ready, just like a standard kitchen oven, and you seldom if ever torch your dinner or your eyebrows. With an open grill, you must keep an eye on the food, turn it every few minutes, and move it around as necessary to avoid flare-ups. You must control the intensity of the fire and keep track of time well enough to gauge doneness. Some grill industry promoters say this is just too difficult for an American backyard cook, although it's how people grill at home everywhere else in the world. Personally, we like to be fully involved in the cooking, but even if we didn't, the flavor trade-off would make the slight extra effort worthwhile.

Covered cooking on a grill does make sense in stormy weather, and in some cases when you want to bake or roast food outside. Just because you're using a grill in these situations, however, doesn't mean that you're grilling. You can bake a cake in any covered grill that will maintain a steady temperature, but it won't be a grilled cake. We stick with actual grilling in this book, except in the chapter on rotisserie roasting—a kindred method of cooking for cuts of meat too large to grill.

TIME AND TEMPERATURE

Interviewers constantly ask us about the most common mistake people make in grilling. Our answer sounds strange perhaps, but it's true: we forget that we're cooking. We're enjoying the outdoors, spending time with family and friends, and imbibing our favorite libation. It's easy to neglect the basic correlates of all cooking: time and temperature. To cook anything well in any way, you apply a proper level of heat for the right period of time. Too often when we're grilling we don't regulate the intensity of the fire or adjust it appropriately for different foods, and we judge the cooking time by how long it takes to drink a beer.

That approach works to some extent with forgiving foods such as hamburgers and hot dogs, the first things that most of us grill. With other ingredients, though, it's usually a recipe for disaster. We all understand this working in our kitchens, inside. No one would ever try to bake a pie by guessing about a good temperature and then letting it cook until they're ready for dessert. Outside, we want to play looser, but the same principles still apply.

Controlling the temperature of the fire is essential. Every food grills best at a particular heat level. The only effective way to measure and then maintain that temperature on an open grill is the time-honored hand test that people have used for eons in all forms of cooking. Place your hand a couple of inches over the top of the cooking grate and count the number of seconds until the heat of the fire forces you to pull away. One to two seconds signifies hot, three seconds indicates medium-high, and four to five seconds denotes medium. You seldom grill meat, fish, or poultry at lower temperatures, although some fruits and vegetables thrive at a reduced range of medium-low, which tests out at six to seven seconds.

The hand test may sound a little primitive for our technological age, but it provides a more accurate and universal gauge of heat than any modern gadget made for the grill. The thermometers built into the hood of many grills today register only the oven heat when the cover is closed, not the true grilling temperature right above the fire. In open grilling, those gauges don't measure anything. The temperature knobs on gas grills marked "hot," "medium," and "low" may provide more help over time, but not until you've determined how those settings compare with your hand measurements.

Use the hand test on both charcoal and gas fires to establish an appropriate heat level before you begin grilling. Temperature adjustments are simple on gas grills, of course, and not much more difficult on charcoal models. With a charcoal grill, fine-tune the heat level by adding or removing coals, opening or closing vents, or moving the fire closer to the food, depending on the design of your grill. An adjustable firebox makes the task particularly easy, but even on a standard kettle-style grill, you can rev up or dampen the fire effectively by varying the quantity of charcoal and the amount of air getting to the coals through the bottom vents.

Thick steaks, some other cuts of red meat, and a few other foods grill best on a two-level fire, usually starting for a few minutes on high heat and finishing on medium. On gas grills with three or more burners, you can usually keep a hot fire and a medium fire going simultaneously from the beginning, and on smaller models, you simply turn down the heat at the appropriate point. On charcoal grills, you establish two different cooking areas, one with coals in a single layer for moderate heat and another with coals piled two to three deep for a hot fire.

We grill at home with both gas and charcoal, and find little difference in the results most of the time. Unlike charcoal counterparts, some open gas grills don't get hot enough to properly sear steaks, but they generally work fine with foods that prefer a moderate fire, such as chicken and vegetables. Infrared gas grills and new LP (liquid propane) models with an infrared burner or searing station possess plenty of firepower for any purpose, and offer an even greater temperature range than charcoal.

For us, the choice between the fuels is mainly a matter of moods. We choose gas for everyday grilling because of its speed and convenience, and change to charcoal or wood for entertaining to create a more casual, relaxed party atmosphere. If you don't want to deal with more than one grill, pick the kind that fits you, your purposes, and your budget.

OTHER GRILLING TIPS AND TRICKS

Cooking open with direct heat, tending your fire, and watching the food and the time: these are the basics of good grilling. There are other important steps toward success, however, which can make a significant difference in your neighborhood renown.

- **Think Grate.** Before you put food on a grill, make sure that the cooking grate is clean, hot, and lightly oiled. Preheat the grate, with the cover down, for up to fifteen minutes to get it hot. Raise the cover and measure the temperature above the grate with the hand test, adjusting the heat as necessary to the most appropriate level for the food you're grilling. Then carefully brush the grate with a thin coat of oil, applied with a cloth or a kitchen brush; don't spray oil on the grill or use excessive amounts, which will cause flare-ups. When you're finished cooking, scrape the grate clean with a wire brush or nylon scrubber before it cools.

- **Ready, Set, Go.** Before any guests arrive, gather and lay out everything you will need for grilling. Once the cooking starts, you won't have time to scurry around in search of ingredients, tools, towels, or anything else.

- **Time the Grilling.** Decide in advance how long you expect to be cooking the food, checking a recipe for the information if needed. Then set a timer to alert you to turn the food or check it for doneness. Carry a small, inexpensive pocket timer with you.

• Check for Doneness. If you're grilling a large cut of meat, fish, or poultry, use an instant-read meat thermometer to check for doneness, taking care that the probe doesn't touch bone. With food that's too thin for a thermometer to register well, such as boneless chicken breast, cut into the meat when you think it's ready to make sure the center is cooked through.

• Long and Strong Tools. The only tools you need for grilling—other than a timer and an instant-read meat thermometer—are long and strong spatulas and tongs for turning food. Everything else is merely a frill.

• Control Flare-Ups. When dripping fat produces a leaping flame under the food, move your vittles to a different part of the grate, at least temporarily. You don't want burned food. Reduce the odds of flare-ups in advance by maintaining a clean grate, cutting excess fat from meat, and keeping oil in marinades to a minimum.

Little Hot Numbers

Nothing warms up a casual outdoor grill party like some hot nibbles from the grill. Served with a cold brew, chilled white or rosé wine, or an iced drink, they draw people together around the food and whet the appetite for everything to come. Each of our choices—from sizzling steak wrapped in lettuce leaves to oysters with Tabasco vinaigrette—grills quickly and is easy to prep and serve.

You don't need to offer more than one of the starters for a regular dinner party, supplemented perhaps with some olives, an assortment of raw vegetables with a dip, salted nuts, or chips and salsa. On the other hand, you can serve several as a complete meal for a grazing party while your friends stand and chat. Fire up the tidbits and lay them out for guests in two or three successive courses, interspersed with other pre-prepared finger food. Whether as a tapas-style plate for grazing, or as a standard appetizer, these high-stepping little numbers rev up both the taste buds and the vibes.

LETTUCE WRAPS WITH ASIAN STEAK

Everyone loves lettuce wraps—ubiquitous these days on upscale restaurant menus—and they provide a good way to involve your guests in assembling the meal. They even work as a main course, served four to six per guest with steaming white rice or long egg noodles and some store-bought Asian peanut or ginger sauce.

Makes 24 wraps

MARINADE

¾ cup soy sauce

¼ cup rice vinegar

2½ tablespoons sugar

2 tablespoons minced fresh ginger

1 tablespoon Asian toasted sesame oil

1 teaspoon Asian chile paste

3 garlic cloves, minced

3 scallions, roots and limp tops trimmed, chopped

1½ pounds flank steak

1 ripe mango, peeled and sliced in thin strips, or 1 or 2 tangy apples, sliced in thin strips

1 small red onion, sliced in thin strips

3 tablespoons fresh lime juice

Approximately 24 crisp butter, Bibb, or romaine lettuce leaves

2 tablespoons sesame seeds, toasted

Stir together the marinade ingredients in a small bowl. Set aside about one quarter of the marinade. Place the steak in a zippered plastic bag and pour the larger portion of marinade over it. Seal and toss back and forth to distribute the marinade. Let sit at room temperature for 30 minutes while you prepare the grill.

Fire up the grill, bringing the heat to high (1 to 2 seconds with the hand test).

Drain the steak. Grill it over high heat for about 3 to 4 minutes per side, until well-seared on the surface but still pink at the center.

Let the steak sit for 5 minutes. Meanwhile, toss together the mango, onion, and lime juice in a medium bowl. Slice the steak across the grain very thinly, into strips no more than ¼ inch in thickness. Cut the strips into thirds. Toss the steak with the reserved marinade and arrange on a platter. Surround with a plate of lettuce leaves, the mango mixture, and the sesame seeds. To assemble, let guests spoon about ¼ cup of the steak onto each lettuce leaf. Top with portions of the mango mixture. Sprinkle with sesame seeds and enjoy.

Adding a Personal Signature:

For those who don't eat red meat, substitute grilled chicken breast for the steak or even firm tofu, using the same marinade.

Replace the Asian marinade with one of these made with store-bought sauces:

Caribbean jerk sauce. Mix ¾ cup of bottled jerk sauce with ¼ cup lime juice.

Bottled balsamic vinaigrette. Skip the sesame seed garnish.

Piri piri sauce. Mix about ¾ cup of bottled piri piri sauce, ¼ cup lemon juice, and 1 tablespoon sugar. Substitute chopped peanuts for the sesame seeds.

ASIAN BUFFET

Lettuce Wraps with Asian Steak

Tangy Thai Chicken (page 98)

White rice, served from a large bamboo steamer

Ginger Blondies (page 169)

ZESTY PORTOBELLO WEDGES

We got this unusual seasoning idea from Chef Jack Czarnecki, a true master of the mushroom. To dress it up for a grazing party, garnish individual plates with a few tender greens tossed with vinaigrette, dollops of garlic mayonnaise, and perhaps a couple of halved tiny tomatoes for additional color.

Makes about 24 wedges

3 tablespoons butter

3 tablespoons Chinese oyster sauce

1 or 2 canned chipotle chiles, minced, with 2 tablespoons of adobo sauce from the can, or 3 to 4 tablespoons chipotle ketchup

6 large, fleshy portobello mushroom caps

About 2 dozen baguette slices

1 plump garlic clove, halved

Minced scallion greens

Warm the butter in a small pan. When melted, mix in the oyster sauce and chile and its liquid. If too thick to spread easily, add a bit of water. Brush the mushrooms with the mixture on all surfaces and let sit for 20 to 30 minutes.

Fire up the grill, bringing the heat to medium (4 to 5 seconds with the hand test).

Arrange the mushrooms on the grill cap side up, to caramelize some of the juices on their undersides immediately. Cook for a total of 8 to 10 minutes, turning the mushrooms at least twice. Toast the baguette slices at the edge of the grill at the same time, turning once. Rub the baguette slices with the cut side of the garlic clove.

Slice each mushroom into four wedges. Serve on a platter or small plates, sprinkled with the scallion greens for color, with the baguette slices on the side. The wedges are good warm or at room temperature.

GOAT CHEESE WRAPPED IN GRAPE LEAVES

For a classy combination of earthy presentation and elegant flavor, nothing beats softened, tangy goat cheese served in charred grape leaves.

Serves 6

5- to 7-ounce round or log fresh goat cheese

4 to 6 large grape leaves (from a jar), rinsed

2 teaspoons extra virgin olive oil

1 tablespoon minced fresh herbs, such as chives, oregano, or thyme, optional

Diced tomato, caper berries, and briny green or black olives or a combination

Crackers or small toasts

Arrange the grape leaves more or less into a circle, overlapping the leaves enough to cover any holes. You want a solid wrapper of leaves. Place the cheese in the center of the leaves. Pour 1 teaspoon of the oil over the cheese and sprinkle with herbs if you like. Wrap the leaves up over the cheese, covering it completely. Coat the package with the remaining oil.

Fire up the grill, bringing the temperature to medium (4 to 5 seconds with the hand test).

Grill the cheese for 6 to 8 minutes, turning on all sides, until soft but short of oozing out of the protective wrap of semi-charred leaves.

Transfer the cheese to a platter. Fold the grape leaves back from the top of the cheese. Scatter the tomato, capers, and olives around the cheese and fill the remaining portion of the platter with crackers.

GRILLED PEARS WITH SERRANO HAM AND CABRALES BLUE CRUMBLES

This tasty appetizer pays homage to the Spanish tapas tradition, a great way to entertain.

Serves 4 to 8

4 ripe medium pears, peeled, halved and cored

¼ cup walnut oil

3 tablespoons brown sugar

½ pound crumbled Cabrales or other soft blue cheese

8 paper-thin slices serrano ham, other Spanish ham, or prosciutto

A handful of mixed greens, optional

Sherry vinegar or red wine vinegar

Place the pears in a shallow dish. Pour the oil over the pears and turn them to coat evenly. Sprinkle with the brown sugar and let sit while you prepare the grill.

Fire up the grill, bringing the heat to medium (4 to 5 seconds with the hand test).

Drain the pears, reserving the oil-sugar mixture.

Arrange the pears on the grill cut side down. Grill the pears over medium heat for 8 to 10 minutes, turning once. Drizzle a little of the oil-sugar mixture into the cavities of the pears. If you plan to serve immediately, sprinkle them with the cheese and remove from the grill. Serve on individual plates while the pears are still warm and the cheese soft, beside nicely arranged ham slices and a few green leaves, if you like. Alternately, let the pears cool, then add the cheese crumbles and arrange the ham. In either case, drizzle with just a bit of the vinegar right before serving.

BITE-SIZE CHICKEN KEBABS

Small skewers of food make versatile appetizers. Add or subtract ingredients depending on what else you're serving. Opt for more vegetables when the other courses are hearty, or more chicken with a salad supper.

Juice and minced zest of 2 lemons

3 tablespoons flavorful olive oil

2 tablespoons coarse-grain prepared mustard

1 teaspoon Worcestershire sauce

½ teaspoon sweet paprika

KEBABS

½ pound boneless, skinless chicken breast, cut into ½-inch cubes

2 to 3 cups bite-size mixed vegetable chunks such as red onions, scallions, zucchini, tiny tomatoes, and/or button mushrooms

½ cup pitted green olives

1 lemon, cut into ¼-inch-thick slices, each slice cut into four pie-shaped wedges

Soaked bamboo skewers, preferably 6 to 10 inches in length

Coarse salt, either kosher or sea salt

Flavorful olive oil, optional

In a small bowl, mix together the lemon juice, oil, mustard, Worcestershire, and paprika.

Fire up the grill, bringing the heat to medium (4 to 5 seconds with the hand test).

While the grill heats, thread just a couple of bites' worth of chicken, vegetables, olives, and lemons on each skewer, avoiding crowding. Brush with the lemon juice mixture and reserve the rest. Sprinkle with salt.

Even soaked bamboo skewers can burn before the food is done if exposed to direct heat. To avoid turning the skewers into kindling, arrange their handles off of the heat as much as possible. If the cooking grate is below the surface of the grill, as in a charcoal kettle model, slide a strip of foil under the handles to deflect the heat.

Grill over medium heat for 6 to 8 minutes, turning to cook on all sides. Brush all over with the reserved marinade after about 5 minutes. When done, the chicken should be firm and white, and the vegetables tender with a few crisp edges. Sprinkle with the lemon zest. If serving from plates, you may want to pour just a touch of olive oil over the kebabs.

Adding a Personal Signature:

We often intersperse among the other ingredients small bits of a cheese that softens but doesn't melt. Use about ½ pound Haloumi, queso blanco, or panela cheese, cut into ½-inch cubes. The slightly chewy texture provides a perfect foil for tender vegetables, chicken, and fish.

Replace the chicken with similar size pieces of other proteins, such as:

- swordfish steak

- pork tenderloin

- lamb loin.

SAUSAGES AND BABY ONIONS
WITH THREE MUSTARDS

Few aromas tantalize an appreciative audience more than onions and sausages browning over a fire. After grilling, simply slice the sausages into rounds, mound everything high on a platter, add a selection of mustards, and let your guests help themselves with picks or small bamboo skewers.

Serves up to 8 as an appetizer

2 pounds or more mixed uncooked sausages, such as well-seasoned bratwurst, spicy Italian, garlicky knockwurst, and a chicken- or turkey-based sausage (preferably 5 to 6 ounces each)

1 to 2 bunches Mexican green onions (baby onions on the stem), or large scallions, roots and limp tops trimmed

Vegetable oil

Small pots of three mustards of contrasting styles or flavors, at least one coarse grain

Fire up the grill for a two-level fire capable of cooking first on high heat (1 to 2 seconds with the hand test) and then on medium heat (4 to 5 seconds with the hand test).

Grill the sausages for a total of 15 to 20 minutes. Soft-textured, freshly-made market sausages generally cook in the shorter amount of time, with denser, commercially-made links taking longer. Arrange the sausages over high heat and grill for about 6 minutes, rolling periodically to crisp on all sides. Move the sausages to medium heat and continue cooking for 10 to 15 minutes. If your sausages are larger, add a couple of minutes to the cooking time over medium heat. If smaller, subtract a couple of minutes over high heat. When done, the sausages should be brown, plump, and still juicy.

Rub the onions with oil and grill them over the medium fire, with their tops angled toward the coolest portion of the grill. Cook 6 to 12 minutes, depending on size, until tender with a few brown spots.

Let the sausages sit for a couple of minutes, then slice into bite-size rounds. Arrange on a platter with the uncut onions, place the mustards nearby, and let guests help themselves with picks or skewers.

Adding a Personal Signature:

Make the platter more elaborate by adding slices of fully pre-cooked sausages to the grilled varieties. Good options include salami or pepperoni, a French saucisson, or Spanish chorizo (also sold uncooked, so make sure you know which you're getting).

Grill hot and sweet Italian sausages, along with fennel slices or halved endives that have been brushed with oil and grilled with the sausages when they are on medium heat. Use the vegetables as a bed for the meat.

GRILL-ROASTED OYSTERS
WITH TABASCO VINAIGRETTE

Grilled oysters may strike friends as exotic, but few things are easier to master. They pop open over the fire, eliminating any shucking, and require only a simple dressing to accentuate their natural flavor. Buy a few extra oysters to avoid disappointment if one or more doesn't open. We've never seen them go to waste.

Makes 24 oysters, serving 4 or more

VINAIGRETTE

½ cup plus 1 tablespoon vegetable oil, preferably corn oil

3 tablespoons white vinegar

1 teaspoon Tabasco sauce, or more to taste

Coarse salt, either kosher or sea salt

Freshly cracked pepper

24 fresh oysters in their shells, scrubbed, preferably smaller oysters with somewhat flat shells

Rock salt, raw rice, seaweed, a platter's worth of fresh herb sprigs, or a couple of clean dishtowels

Fire up the grill, bringing the heat to high (1 to 2 seconds with the hand test).

Whisk together the vinaigrette ingredients in a small bowl.

Arrange the oysters in a single layer on the grill grate, deeper shells down. If they don't all fit, place as many on the grill as you can and then add those remaining as you remove ones that are done. Roast the oysters about 5 to 10 minutes, taking them off with sturdy tongs as soon as each one pops yawningly open. They burble and sputter a bit as they cook. After 10 minutes, remove any remaining unopened oysters and discard them.

That's all we do, leaving the top shells in place for serving so the guests can pop out the oysters with a fork.

Arrange the oysters on plates or one big platter, on a bed of rock salt to hold them upright to retain their juices. Spoon in a little of the vinaigrette and serve more on the side. Eat as soon as the shells are cool enough for the guests to handle, slurping as you go. Remind your guests to not eat the rock salt.

Adding a Personal Signature:

For a more robust dish, replace the vinaigrette with a richer BBQ butter. Melt together in a small pan over the grill or stove: ½ cup (1 stick) butter, 2 tablespoons tomato-based barbecue sauce, a few splashes of Tabasco or other hot sauce, and a couple of good grindings of pepper. Mix well before spooning into the oysters.

MENU FOR A SOUTHERN SHORE SUPPER

Grill-Roasted Oysters with Tabasco Vinaigrette

Smoky Dry-Rubbed Shrimp (page 114)

American Heartland Platter (page 40)

Peach pie or cobbler

Made-to-Order
Grilled Pizzas

Grilled pizzas are ideal fare for a casual outdoor party. The pies taste great because grilling emulates the high-fire cooking process of a professional wood-burning pizza oven. You must tend the cooking carefully, rotating the pizzas on the grill, but you'll dazzle your friends while you do it as if you were twirling a crust in the air. Offer a broad choice of toppings so guests can design their own masterpieces. Everyone will be boasting about their creation, passing around bites, and celebrating your inspired idea.

The cooking process is easy, at least on grills with a moderately large cooking grate positioned at the top of the grill. On charcoal kettle-style grills and other models that feature a grate set down inside the grill, the cooking is more of a challenge because of the need to rotate the pizzas, but you can handle the task if you're set on success. The rotation is necessary because pizza requires a two-level fire, hot in one area and medium-low in another. The pizza dough is initially placed over the hot fire, directly on the grate without a pan, until the dough stiffens. Then you flip the crust, add toppings, and complete the cooking with half of the pizza over the hot fire and the other half over the medium-low fire, rotating it as the sides brown.

The process may sound a little complicated, but our five-year-old grandson mastered the basics well enough to serve as an able assistant at a recent neighborhood party. Practice it a couple of times in advance of your first performance and you'll be parading out for encores for years to come.

PIZZA MARGHERITA WITH FIRE-ROASTED TOMATO SAUCE

This red, white, and green Italian classic stands on a par with any other pizza ever made. It highlights the texture and grill flavor of the crust and makes a scrumptious base for other toppings. Just avoid using a heavy hand with the tomato sauce and other ingredients. Grilled pizzas taste best, and are much easier to maneuver and eat, when you go relatively light on the toppings.

Makes two 11-inch pizzas, enough for 4 main dish servings

FIRE-ROASTED TOMATO SAUCE

3 red-ripe plum tomatoes

2 tablespoons tomato paste

2 tablespoons chopped fresh basil

1 tablespoon flavorful olive oil

Splash or two of garlic-flavored oil, optional

Salt

One recipe Pizza Dough (page 34)

1¼ cups shredded mozzarella

Pinch or two of crushed dried hot red chile, optional

½ cup lightly-packed thin-sliced fresh basil leaves

Fire up the grill for a two-level fire capable of cooking at the same time on both high heat (1 to 2 seconds with the hand test) and medium-low heat (6 seconds with the hand test).

Grill the tomatoes over high heat about 6 to 8 minutes, turning on all sides, until the skins are somewhat blackened and split and the tomatoes are soft. As soon as the tomatoes are cool enough to handle, halve them and squeeze out the watery liquid. Puree the tomatoes in a blender or food processor with the remaining sauce ingredients.

Place the toppings within easy reach of the grill. The process must go quickly once you begin cooking. Have a baking sheet near the grill on a convenient work surface and keep a large spatula or pizza peel handy.

Place the first crust on the grill, laying it directly on the cooking grate. Grill uncovered over high heat for 1 to 1½ minutes, until the crust becomes firm yet still flexible. Don't worry about any bubbles that form

on the crust, as they will flatten when you turn over the crust in the next step.

Flip the crust onto the baking sheet, cooked side up. Immediately spoon on half of the tomato sauce, sprinkle with half of the cheese, and a bit of chile if you wish. Quickly return the pizza to the grate (without the baking sheet), uncooked side down. Arrange the pie so that half of it is over high heat and the other half is over medium-low. Cook the pizza another 3 to 5 minutes, rotating it in quarter turns about every 30 to 45 seconds. This may sound awkward but becomes second nature very quickly. Using the spatula to lift the edge slightly, check the bottom during the last minute or two, rotating a bit faster or slower as needed to get a uniformly brown, crisp crust. Scatter with basil shortly before removing the pizza from the grill.

Slice the pizza into wedges and serve immediately. Repeat the process for your second pizza.

Adding a Personal Signature:

Some options for additional toppings include:

- a selection of other cheeses, such as buttery fontina or Gouda, mellow Asiago, tangy ricotta salata or blue cheese, or nutty Parmesan or Gruyère

- capers or large caper berries

- green and black olives

- arugula leaves

- paper-thin garlic slices

- sautéed fennel slices and a sprinkling of fennel seeds.

MEAT-LOVER'S PIZZA

With pizzas featuring meat, we prefer to use fresh tomato slices as a base, rather than a sauce, because the meat flavors stand out better. Any of the meats that are refrigerated should be brought to inside room temperature for twenty to thirty minutes before you plan to use them so that they warm thoroughly on the grill.

Makes two 11-inch pizzas, enough for 4 main dish servings

2 or 3 red-ripe plum tomatoes

2 teaspoons olive oil

Salt

1¼ cups shredded mozzarella

¼ cup grated Pecorino Romano or Parmesan

2 tablespoons minced fresh basil or 1 tablespoon minced fresh sage or 2 teaspoons crumbled dried basil or 1 teaspoon crumbled dried sage

One recipe Pizza Dough (page 34)

½ to ¾ pound cooked meat, crumbled or sliced, at least two kinds (choose from the signature options or other personal favorites)

Fire up the grill for a two-level fire capable of cooking at the same time on both high heat (1 to 2 seconds with the hand test) and medium-low heat (6 seconds with the hand test).

Halve the tomatoes lengthwise, and then squeeze out the liquid, which would make the pizza soggy. Dice the tomatoes, then toss with the oil and salt. Stir the mozzarella, Pecorino, and basil together in a small, separate bowl.

Place the toppings within easy reach of the grill. The process must go quickly once you begin cooking. Have a baking sheet near the grill on a convenient work surface and keep a large spatula or pizza peel handy.

Place the first crust on the grill, laying it directly on the cooking grate. Grill uncovered over high heat for 1 to 1½ minutes, until the crust becomes firm yet still flexible. Don't worry about any bubbles that form on the crust, as they will flatten when you turn over the crust in the next step.

Flip the crust onto the baking sheet, cooked side up. Immediately sprinkle with half of the cheese mixture, spoon on half of the tomatoes, and top with about half of the remaining ingredients, including the meat. Quickly return the pizza to the grill (without the baking sheet), uncooked side down. Arrange the pie so that half of it is over high heat and the other half is over medium-low. Cook the pizza another 3 to 5 minutes, rotating it in quarter turns about every 30 to 45 seconds. This may sound awkward but becomes second nature very quickly. Using the spatula to lift the edge slightly, check the bottom during the last minute or two, rotating a bit faster or slower as needed to get a uniformly brown, crisp crust.

Slice the pizza into wedges and serve immediately. Repeat the process for your second pizza.

Adding a Personal Signature:

Lay out a hearty variety of thinly sliced meats for your friends to select for themselves. Some of the best options include:

- pepperoni
- grilled Italian sausage
- prosciutto or serrano ham
- capocollo
- Canadian bacon
- slices of simply seasoned leftover steak or Classic Crusty Pork Tenderloin (page 74).

Offer a few non-meat additions as well, such as:

- slivered pickled pepperoncini peppers
- grilled bell pepper slices
- sautéed onions or mushrooms
- chopped roasted mild green chile, our favorite.

SUPER BOWL SUNDAY SUPPER

Antipasto Extravaganza (page 38)

Meat-Lover's Pizzas

Ice Cream Sundae Dessert Bar (page 173)

WHITE PIZZA

Different enough to seem special, but not far from anyone's comfort zone, white pizza omits the standard tomato sauce, substituting silky crème fraîche in this case. Sour cream sometimes makes an adequate substitute for crème fraîche, but not here, where it could break down under the high heat. This style of pizza is really good served with a cruet of spicy olive oil for drizzling.

Makes two 11-inch pizzas, enough for 4 servings

¾ cup crème fraîche, at room temperature

¼ cup grated Parmesan

One recipe Pizza Dough (page 34)

2 teaspoons olive oil

⅓ cup slivered strong-flavored black olives, either brine- or oil-cured

½ cup drained, sliced marinated artichoke hearts, optional

Fire up the grill for a two-level fire capable of cooking at the same time on both high heat (1 to 2 seconds with the hand test) and medium-low heat (6 seconds with the hand test).

Stir together the crème fraîche with the Parmesan. Reserve at room temperature.

Place the toppings within easy reach of the grill. The process must go quickly once you begin cooking. Have a baking sheet near the grill on a convenient work surface and keep a large spatula or pizza peel handy.

Place the first crust on the grill, laying it directly on the cooking grate. Grill uncovered over high heat for 1 to 1½ minutes, until the crust becomes firm yet still flexible. Don't worry about any bubbles that form on the crust, as they will flatten when you turn over the crust in the next step.

Flip the crust onto the baking sheet, cooked side up. Immediately spoon on half of the oil, smearing it around. Then spoon on half of the crème fraîche mixture, and top with half of the remaining ingredients. Quickly return the pizza to the grill (without the baking sheet), uncooked side down. Arrange the pie so that half of it is over high heat and the other half is over medium-low. Cook the pizza another 3 to 5 minutes, rotating it in quarter turns about every 30 to 45 seconds. This may sound awkward but becomes second nature very quickly. Using the spatula to lift the edge slightly, check the bottom during the last minute or two, rotating a bit faster or slower as needed to get a uniformly brown, crisp crust.

Slice the pizza into wedges and serve immediately. Repeat the process for your second pizza.

Adding a Personal Signature:

Since you're starting with a less familiar style of pizza, you've already scored big points as hosts and don't need to offer a large array of additional topping options. Concentrate on a few choices that reinforce your cutting-edge image, such as:

- **an egg** (fairly common on pizzas in Europe) cracked into a cup and poured over the other toppings just after you return the pizza to the grill; cover the grill if necessary to cook the egg to the desired doneness with additional reflected heat from the top.

- **mascarpone or fromage blanc**

- **diced or sliced Canadian bacon or ham, or crisp bacon crumbles**, the best meats for this type of pizza.

PIZZA DOUGH

The crust for a grilled pizza should be a supporting player of importance, not just a lackluster base for a pile of toppings. You could use a store bought crust, but we've never found one that gives us the crispy, crunchy, flavorsome results that come from this homemade dough.

Makes two thin 11-inch pizza crusts

2 cups flour, preferably bread flour, or all-purpose (more as needed)	1 teaspoon rapid-rise yeast, such as Fleischmann's
3 tablespoons cornmeal, preferably coarse ground	¾ cup lukewarm water
1 teaspoon salt	2 tablespoons plus 1 teaspoon olive oil

In a food processor, pulse together the flour, cornmeal, salt, and yeast. With the motor running, add the water and the 2 tablespoons of oil. Continue processing for about 30 seconds more, until the dough forms a cohesive ball that is smooth and elastic. If it remains sticky, add another tablespoon or two of flour.

Knead the dough a few times on a floured work surface, forming it into a ball. Pour the remaining oil into a large bowl and add the dough, turning it around and over until coated with oil. Cover with a damp cloth. Set the dough in a warm, draft-free spot and let it rise until doubled, about 1 hour. Punch the dough down. Form the dough into two thin disks, each about ⅛ inch thick and 11 inches in diameter. We find a combination of first flattening the crust with a rolling pin and then stretching and prodding it with fingers works best. (A raised edge isn't necessary.)

The dough is ready to use at this point, but also can be saved for later in the refrigerator or freezer. Stack the crusts on a baking sheet covered with wax paper, with a sheet of wax paper between the crusts. If refrigerating or freezing, chill the crusts on the baking sheet for about 30 minutes to firm the dough, then remove from the baking sheet and wrap the crusts before storing. Bring the crusts back to room temperature before proceeding.

Grilled
Platters

Grilling may have developed as a means to cook meat, but it does wonders on many vegetables as well. A colorful platter of grilled, mixed vegetables is a striking and festive centerpiece for any gathering of friends, whether offered as an appetizer, main course, salad, or side dish. You can serve the veggies at room temperature, allowing you to prepare them in advance.

The grilling couldn't be easier. Most vegetables cook best on medium heat—so you don't need the hot fire required by many meats—and you can forget concerns about doneness, simply grilling until everything feels appropriately tender to you. Except for bell peppers and chiles, where the skin protects the interior and is stripped off before eating, oil or butter vegetables or brush them with vinaigrette in advance to keep them from drying out on the grill. A breeze to cook and a veritable cornucopia on the table, any of these platters may make the hosts the happiest people at a party.

ANTIPASTO EXTRAVAGANZA

Nothing to it. Just bathe the vegetables in a simple vinaigrette, grill them a couple of hours before the company comes, and top them with a tomato relish at the last minute. If you've never tried an especially coarse and flaky salt, such as Maldon sea salt, give it a go here. It looks beautiful and the taste is a revelation.

Serves 6 or more

VINAIGRETTE

½ cup plus 1 tablespoon flavorful olive oil

3 tablespoons white wine vinegar

1 garlic clove, minced

¼ teaspoon Dijon mustard

Salt

Freshly milled pepper

1 large red, orange, or yellow bell pepper

1 large red onion, cut into ½-inch-thick slices

1 eggplant, about 1 pound, sliced into ⅓- to ½-inch-thick rounds

2 or 3 small heads radicchio, quartered through the stem end, or 4 to 6 endives, halved through the stem end

1 small, trimmed fennel bulb, cut into ⅓- to ½-inch-thick slices through the stem end

1 zucchini, about ½ pound, sliced into ⅓- to ½-inch-thick rounds

2 or 3 red-ripe plum tomatoes, halved lengthwise

RELISH

2 red-ripe plum tomatoes, finely diced

2 tablespoons minced fresh basil or flat-leaf parsley

1 tablespoon flavorful olive oil

Flaky sea salt, such as Maldon or coarse salt, either kosher or sea salt

Flaky sea salt, such as Maldon, or coarse salt, either kosher or sea salt

Capers, caper berries, green or black olives, or Parmesan curls (made with a vegetable peeler), optional

Whisk together the vinaigrette ingredients in a small bowl.

Run a thin metal skewer through each onion slice to hold it together. Brush the vegetables with about three-quarters of the vinaigrette. Give the eggplant the heaviest coat.

Fire up the grill, bringing the temperature to medium (4 to 5 seconds with the hand test).

Grill the vegetables, in batches if necessary. Plan on grilling times of 12 to 15 minutes for the pepper and the onion slices, 8 to 12 minutes for the eggplant, radicchio, and fennel, 6 to 8 minutes for the zucchini, and 4 to 6 minutes for the tomatoes. Arrange the tomatoes cut side down first. Turn the pepper on all sides to cook evenly, and the rest of the vegetables three times, brushing all with the remaining vinaigrette as they cook. Cook until tender, removing each vegetable as it is done.

Transfer the pepper to a plastic bag and close to let it steam and loosen the skin. When cool enough to handle, pull off any loose charred pieces of skin. Slice the pepper into thin strips, discarding the seeds and stem.

Arrange the vegetables attractively on a platter. Serve warm or at room temperature. Just before serving, stir together the tomato relish. Top the platter with the relish, a sprinkling of salt, and any of the optional garnishes.

Adding a Personal Signature:

Transform the antipasto into a full vegetarian meal by layering the vegetables over crusty grilled polenta on individual plates, with a portion of the relish dabbed on each.

Turn the platter into the filling for party panini. Toast some split Italian bread or hearty rolls on the edge of the grill, then spread them with store-bought tapenade, sun-dried tomato compote, or just good olive oil. Stack some of the grilled vegetables, and if you wish, thin slices of mozzarella or provolone cheese between the portions of bread. Cut into manageable portions and serve.

AMERICAN HEARTLAND PLATTER

This hearty combo works particularly well as a side dish with steaks, burgers, and pork tenderloin.

Serves 6 or more

6 red potatoes or other small potatoes, 3 to 4 ounces each, halved

1 large red onion, cut in 6 to 8 wedges

1 large white onion, cut in 6 to 8 wedges

6 ears corn, husked and silks removed, then halved crosswise into two small ears

1 or 2 yellow summer squash, about ½ pound, sliced into ⅓- to ½-inch-thick disks

½ cup (1 stick) butter, melted

Flaky sea salt, such as Maldon, or coarse salt, either kosher or sea salt

Fresh chives, optional

Prepare the vegetables. Par-boil the potatoes in salted water until just tender, about 10 minutes, and drain them. Run a toothpick through each onion wedge to hold it together. Brush all the vegetables with butter, using about one-half of it.

Fire up the grill, bringing the temperature to medium (4 to 5 seconds with the hand test).

Grill the vegetables, in batches if necessary. Plan on grilling times of 20 to 25 minutes for the corn, 12 to 15 minutes for the onion wedges, and 6 to 8 minutes for the potatoes and summer squash. Turn the corn on all sides to cook evenly. Turn the other vegetables three times, brushing all of them with the remaining butter as they cook. Cook the potatoes until nicely browned on all surfaces, and the rest of the vegetables until tender, removing each as it is done.

Arrange the vegetables attractively on a platter. Serve while the corn is still hot. Just before serving, sprinkle with salt, and top the platter with the chives if you wish.

Adding a Personal Signature:

Give the platter a Louisiana accent by rubbing all the vegetables with your favorite Cajun-style dry rub or spice blend. Add the rub to taste after you've brushed everything with butter, skipping the salt later unless your blend is salt-free.

ASIAN APPETIZER PLATTER

For this Asian-inspired platter, we use a light mirin and orange dressing over the vegetables. Feel free to mix and match vegetables from this and other platters, or grill just a few rather than all our recommendations, depending on what looks good at the market and how simple you want to keep the meal.

Serves 6 or more

VINAIGRETTE

¼ cup mirin (sweet Japanese rice wine)

¼ cup fresh orange juice

2 tablespoons vegetable oil

½ teaspoon roasted sesame oil

2 teaspoons rice vinegar or white vinegar

Salt

1 eggplant, about 1 pound, sliced lengthwise into 8 to 12 spears, or 4 to 6 small slim Japanese eggplants, halved lengthwise

6 ounces (about 12) medium-thick asparagus spears, trimmed of tough ends

1 large orange, cut into 6 wedges

3 or 4 baby bok choy, halved lengthwise through the stem end, optional

6 scallions, roots and limp tops trimmed

2 large portobello mushroom caps, cut into ⅓- to ½-inch-thick slices

Sesame seeds, minced cilantro, or both

Whisk together the vinaigrette ingredients in a small bowl.

Prepare the vegetables and orange wedges, brushing them with about three-quarters of the vinaigrette. Give the eggplant and mushroom slices the heaviest coat.

Fire up the grill, bringing the temperature to medium (4 to 5 seconds with the hand test).

Grill the vegetables and orange wedges, in batches if necessary. Plan on grilling times of 8 to 12 minutes for the eggplant, 5 to 7 minutes for the asparagus, orange wedges, and bok choy, and 4 to 5 minutes for the scallions and mushroom slices. Turn the vegetables and orange wedges three times, brushing with the remaining vinaigrette as they cook. Cook until tender, removing each as it is done.

Arrange the vegetables and orange wedges attractively on a platter. Serve warm or at room temperature. Just before serving, top the platter with the sesame seeds or cilantro.

MEDITERRANEAN-MEXICAN PEPPER PLATTER

Bell peppers and chiles shine on the grill, taking on the distinctive flavor of the fire as well as or better than any other vegetables. They're at their best when cooked long enough to get good and soft, not simply charred on the surface. You can dress this platter simply with a splash or two of vegetable oil and lime juice, but the pureed salsa introduces additional color and zest to the dish.

Serves 6 or more

SALSA

One drained 12-ounce jar Spanish piquillo peppers, or roasted red bell peppers with 2 pinches of cayenne

1 tablespoon flavorful olive oil

1 garlic clove

1 teaspoon red or white wine vinegar, or sherry vinegar

Salt

Freshly milled pepper

Pinch of sugar, optional

2 plump yellow or orange bell peppers, or a combination

1 red bell pepper

1 green bell pepper

2 or 3 poblano or New Mexican green chiles, or other large mild fresh chiles

A handful of small sweet peppers or chiles, in varied colors, optional

1 ear corn, optional

Olive oil, optional

Crumbled queso fresco, cotija, or feta cheese, or curls of Manchego or Idiazabal cheese (made with a vegetable peeler)

Puree the salsa ingredients in a food processor or blender. Reserve.

Fire up the grill, bringing the temperature to medium (4 to 5 seconds with the hand test).

Grill the peppers, chiles, and corn, if using, in batches if necessary. If using the corn, rub it with enough oil to coat and grill it for about 20 minutes. Plan on grilling times of 12 to 15 minutes for the bell peppers, 8 to 12 minutes for the larger chiles, and 4 to 7 minutes for the small peppers and chiles. Some particularly heavy, thick-walled peppers can take up to 5 minutes longer. Turn the vegetables on all sides, to cook the corn and to darken and blister the pepper and chile skins. Grill the vegetables until tender, removing each as it is done. As the peppers and chiles come off the grill, place them in a plastic bag to steam. When cool enough to handle, strip all the loose skin from them, rinsing your fingers, rather than the pods, as you go.

Slice the peppers and chiles into thick or thin ribbons, collecting all the juices. If you included corn, slice the kernels off the cob. Arrange the ribbons attractively on a platter, spooning some of the salsa on the platter first if you wish. You can toss all the pepper and chile ribbons and juices into a colorful jumble, or arrange each hue in a different mound. Scatter with corn kernels and spoon on salsa. Top with cheese and serve warm or at room temperature.

Adding a Personal Signature:

Serve as a main course in the form of soft tacos, arranging the strips of peppers and chiles in a warm flour tortilla and topping them with the salsa, a favorite chile sauce, or chile con queso.

GARDEN LUNCH

**Mediterranean-Mexican
Pepper Platter**

Orzo and Zucchini Salad (page 164)

Plump cherries on the stem

Sangria Blanca (page 176)

Serious Steaks

If you want a party specialty that you can make better than any restaurant in town, stake your fortune on steak. For full beef flavor, focus your efforts on strip steaks, rib-eyes, and skirts, each an exceptional cut in its own way and all guaranteed to please the pickiest party guest.

Step one is finding a good source, especially for the more expensive premier steaks. Check out expert butchers and meat-cutters in your area and try some of the best mail order purveyors. Look for well-marbled strips and rib-eyes, at least one inch thick, of prime grade or professionally recommended choice grade. The second essential is a two-level fire on an open grill that's capable of searing steaks first on very high heat and then cooking them through on medium. If you have a gas grill that won't get hot enough with the lid up for the initial searing, invest in a secondary charcoal grill, any of which can generate the necessary firepower. Turn the steaks at least three times, putting each side to the fire twice, and add another turn or two if juice begins to pool on the surface at any time. Season the meat simply, to avoid masking the inherent flavor, and don't cook it beyond medium-rare unless a misguided guest insists. Moderately priced skirt steak is an exception to some of these principles, as noted in the recipes, but if you stick to this simple script for the top cuts, your patio steakhouse will shame all the local wannabes in the next Zagat poll.

STRIP STEAKS WITH WORCESTERSHIRE BUTTER

"Salt and pepper steaks," we sometimes call them. The great steaks from the short loin and the rib section beg away from any other seasoning. These strips from the short loin—sometimes labeled "Kansas City," "New York," or "Delmonico"—are almost as tender as filet cuts from the tenderloin but much meatier in flavor. Some hearty eaters can eat a whole steak, but we usually serve half portions to twice as many people. As rich as they are on their own, we can't resist a final flourish of flavored butter at the table.

Serves 4 to 8

1 tablespoon coarse salt, either kosher or sea salt

2 teaspoons coarsely ground pepper

Four 14- to 16-ounce strip steaks, about 1 to 1¼ inches thick

WORCESTERSHIRE BUTTER

6 tablespoons (¾ stick) butter, preferably unsalted

1 tablespoon Worcestershire sauce

Stir together the salt and pepper and then rub over the steaks on all surfaces. Let the steaks sit at room temperature for about 30 minutes.

Fire up the grill for a two-level fire capable of cooking first on high heat (1 to 2 seconds with the hand test) and then on medium (4 to 5 seconds with the hand test).

Grill the steaks over high heat for 2½ minutes per side. Move the steaks to medium heat, turning them again, and continue grilling for 2½ to 3 minutes per side for medium-rare. Turn the steaks a minimum of three times, but more often if juice begins to form on the surface. Rotate a half-turn each time for crisscross grill marks.

While the steaks finish cooking, melt the butter in a skillet on the edge of the grill. Whisk in the Worcestershire sauce.

Plate the steaks, spoon the melted butter over them, and serve.

Adding a Personal Signature:

Steaks with pronounced beefy flavor, such as rib-eyes and skirts, can gain new dimension from a robust dry rub. Develop your own steak blend using the rub from the recipe and these alternative spice mixtures as models:

- 1 tablespoon coarsely ground pepper, 1 to 1½ teaspoons minced lemon zest, 1 teaspoon coarse salt, ¼ teaspoon ground white pepper

- 1 tablespoon ground dried mild red chile, 1 tablespoon ground dried ancho chile, 1 teaspoon coarse salt, 1 teaspoon ground cumin, ½ teaspoon crumbled dried marjoram, sage, or oregano

- 1 tablespoon hickory-flavored salt, 1 teaspoon coarsely ground black pepper, ½ teaspoon ground white pepper

- 1 tablespoon whole black peppercorns, ½ tablespoon whole pink peppercorns, 1 teaspoon whole white peppercorns, 1 teaspoon coarse salt, ½ teaspoon yellow mustard seeds, ½ teaspoon dried onion flakes, mixed and ground together in a blender or spice mill.

PINEAPPLE, SOY, AND PEPPER SKIRT STEAK

Skirt used to be a "butcher's cut," taken home as a privilege of position because it wasn't plentiful enough to market effectively. Those butchers knew their meat because this is one of the tastiest steaks of all, far superior in beefy flavor to many costlier cuts. You grill skirt a little differently than a strip or rib-eye, because of its thinness, and season it more assertively to complement its brawn. If you've developed a relationship with a good butcher or meat-cutter, ask for the outside skirt, a touch more substantial than the inside counterpart.

Serves 4 or more

2 skirt steaks, 1 to 1¼ pounds each, trimmed of membranes and excess fat

½ cup pineapple juice

¼ cup soy sauce

2 tablespoons chili sauce (the ketchup-style condiment) or ketchup

1 tablespoon Worcestershire sauce

1 teaspoon ground ginger

1 garlic clove, minced

2 to 3 teaspoons coarsely ground pepper

Cut each steak in half crosswise to create two shorter, more manageable sections of meat. Place in a large zippered plastic bag. Combine the pineapple juice, soy sauce, chili sauce, Worcestershire, ginger, and garlic in a small bowl, and pour over the steaks. Seal and toss back and forth to coat evenly with the marinade. Refrigerate for 30 minutes to 1 hour, then drain and discard the marinade.

Let the steaks sit at room temperature uncovered while you prepare the grill. Dab any moisture from the surface with a paper towel. Sprinkle with the pepper and pat it in.

Fire up the grill, bringing the temperature to high (1 to 2 seconds with the hand test).

Grill the meat over high heat for 3 to 4 minutes per side if under ½ inch thick, or 4 to 5 minutes per side for ½ inch or more in thickness, until medium-rare. Turn the steaks once, and more often if juice pools on the surface.

Let the steaks rest, covered with foil, for about 5 minutes before slicing, so that the prodigious juices are redistributed. With the knife at a slight diagonal, cut the steaks across the grain and into thin finger-length strips. Serve immediately.

Adding a Personal Signature:

Turn this into an Asian-style salad. Toss the meat strips with a handful each of fresh basil, mint, and cilantro, and several cups of torn Bibb lettuce. Serve with a bottled ginger or peanut salad dressing or sauce.

FAJITAS *REAL*

Skirt steak gained its fame recently as the original meat for fajitas, a north-of-the-border descendant of the Mexican cowboy dish called *arracheras*. With the toppings grilled together with the steak, fajitas make a great show and provide a festive full meal that you can cook in a matter of minutes. There's a pleasant kick of heat to this version, but if you want to tone it down, skip the Tabasco in the marinade or substitute another bell pepper for the chiles in the vegetable topping.

Serves 6 or more

2 skirt steaks, 1 to 1¼ pounds each, trimmed of membranes and excess fat

MARINADE

One 12-ounce bottle or can of beer, preferably medium-bodied such as Bohemia or Dos Equis

Juice of 3 large limes, about ½ cup

Juice of 1 large orange, about ½ cup

1 tablespoon Tabasco chipotle sauce or Worcestershire sauce

DRY RUB

1½ tablespoons chili powder

1 tablespoon coarse salt, either kosher or sea salt

2 teaspoons ground cumin

2 teaspoons brown sugar

1 large red onion, sliced in 6 to 8 thick wedges

2 red bell peppers

2 poblano chiles, or other fresh mild to medium green chiles

Vegetable oil

Coarse salt, either kosher or sea salt

Guacamole, approximately 1 cup

One or more salsas, approximately 1 cup

12 flour tortillas, warmed

Cut each steak in half crosswise to create two shorter, more manageable sections of meat. Place in a large zippered plastic bag. Combine the beer and citrus juices and pour over the steaks. Seal and toss back and forth to coat evenly with the marinade. Refrigerate for 30 minutes to 1 hour, then drain and discard the marinade.

Let the steaks sit at room temperature uncovered while you prepare the grill. Dab any moisture from the surface with a paper towel. Stir together the dry rub ingredients and massage them into the meat.

Fire up the grill, for a two-level fire capable of cooking on high (1 to 2 seconds with the hand test) and medium heat (4 to 5 seconds with the hand test) at the same time.

Run a toothpick through each onion wedge to hold it together. Coat the bell peppers, chiles, and onion wedges with oil. Arrange them over medium heat and grill until tender, 12 to 15 minutes for the bell peppers and onion wedges and 8 to 12 minutes for the chiles. Turn on all sides and take them off as they are done. Transfer the peppers and chiles to a plastic bag and close to let them steam, loosening the skin. When cool enough to handle, pull off any loose charred skin. Slice the peppers and chiles into thin strips; trim the onion root ends and remove the toothpicks. Toss the vegetables together. Sprinkle with salt and keep warm.

Once the vegetables have been on the grill at least 5 minutes, start cooking the steaks. Grill the steaks 3 to 4 minutes per side if under ½ inch thick, or 4 to 5 minutes per side for ½ inch or more in thickness, until medium-rare. Turn the steaks once, and more often if juice pools on the surface. Let the steaks rest, covered with foil, for about 5 minutes before slicing, so that the juices are redistributed.

With a knife at a slight diagonal, cut the steaks across the grain into thin finger-length strips. To serve, pile the steak strips and vegetable strips on a large platter, offer bowls of guacamole and salsa, and a napkin-lined basket of tortillas. Spoon portions of the steak and vegetables into the tortillas, top with guacamole and salsa, fold up, and feast.

CINCO DE MAYO FAJITAS FIESTA

Margaritas on the rocks

Bottled and canned beer in a tub

Aguas frescas, **such as pureed cantaloupe, honeydew, or watermelon with a splash of orange or lime juice**

Crisp tortilla chips with salsas (one tomato and one another tomatillo)

Fajitas Real

Pinto beans or Corn Pudding (page 166)

Lime sorbet

PEPPER-CRUSTED BONELESS RIB-EYE STEAKS

Cuts from the rib section right in front of the short loin aren't quite as tender as strip steaks, but they trump their neighbors in primal beefy flavor. Rib-eyes—not to be confused with "rib" steaks from an adjoining area— come from the prime rib. Some people like to roast the whole rib, but we much prefer to have it sliced into steaks for grilling, which amplifies the naturally robust essence of the cut. In this case, we start with especially thick steaks for an impressive presentation on a special occasion. Slice them into individual portions at the table as if you were carving a holiday bird.

Serves 6 or more	2 tablespoons freshly cracked pepper 2 tablespoons coarse salt, either kosher or sea salt	Two 1½-pound boneless rib-eye steaks, 2 inches thick

If your pepper mill won't crack pepper coarsely, place peppercorns in a plastic sandwich bag and wack a few times with a mallet for the desired crunchy texture. Stir together the pepper and salt and rub evenly over the steaks. Let the steaks sit at room temperature for 30 to 40 minutes.

Fire up the grill for a two-level fire capable of cooking first on high heat (1 to 2 seconds with the hand test) and then on medium (4 to 5 seconds with the hand test).

Grill the steaks over high heat for 4 minutes per side. Move the steaks to medium heat, turning them again, and continue grilling for 2½ to 3 minutes per side for medium-rare. Turn the steaks a minimum of three times, rotating half-turn each time for crisscross grill marks, but more often if juice begins to form on the surface. The steaks should get very dark and crusty on the surface.

Let the steaks sit covered for 5 minutes, then slice thickly, and serve.

Adding a Personal Signature:

Call us gluttons, but we sometimes grill an extra rib-eye or other fine steak to make deliberate leftovers for super beef sandwiches, good enough for another company meal. Layer thin slices of the steak on a warm toasted roll with crunchy iceberg lettuce, blue cheese crumbles, and Thousand Island dressing spiced up with a little dried ground chile or Tabasco sauce.

FOURTH OF JULY
COOKOUT

**BLT Salad with Warm Bacon Dressing
(page 158)**

**Pepper-Crusted Boneless Rib-Eye
Steaks**

**All-American Barbecued Chicken
Breasts (page 100)**

Corn on the cob

**Mocha Brownie Ice Cream Cake
(page 174)**

Fresh-squeezed lemonade

Burgers *for* All
Occasions

Just because fast-food versions are a worldwide disgrace, don't blame it on the burger. We grill them regularly for our friends—thick, juicy, bragging-rights burgers that anyone would love, from Alaskan lumberjacks to French chefs. Americans perfected the whole idea of the sandwich and we made burgers the icon of our success. Treat them with respect and serve them with pride.

Don't take the fast-food shortcuts, though, or you'll end up with a weenie of a burger. Whether you're working with beef, lamb, turkey, or another main ingredient, make sure it's freshly ground or chopped by you or the meat department, and cook it within a few hours afterward. Season the meat or poultry first, then compact it only lightly to form flat patties that are one-half- to three-quarters-inch thick. Grill beef patties on a two-level fire, starting on high and finishing on medium, and grill most other types of burgers on a steady medium heat. Resist any temptation to squish the burgers with your spatula as you grill, leaving that desiccating trick to the teenage cooks at roadside joints. Eat the burgers immediately, hot off the grill, relishing that distinctive mingling of juicy flavors that makes them the world's premier sandwich.

CLASSIC AT-HOME HAMBURGERS

A two-fisted outdoor delight, this feast in a bun shows why burgers belong at home rather than a drive-up window. Indulge us just once in how we make them. Go to the best meat market in town and order a chunk of beef chuck for hamburger meat, specifying that you want fifteen to twenty percent fat content for the burgers. If you're going to grill within a few hours, get the butcher to grind the chuck for you. If the wait will be longer, grind it yourself at home in a food processor; simply cut the chilled meat into smallish cubes, about one burger's worth at a time, then whir until it's chopped, being sure to avoid pureeing the beef. Cutting back on fat even a little will cut back on flavor a lot, without providing much worthwhile calorie and cholesterol savings. Opting for lighter foods before or afterward makes much more sense to us.

Serves 6 hearty eaters

1 cup mayonnaise

3 tablespoons ketchup or tomato-based barbecue sauce

2¾ pounds freshly ground chuck

1½ teaspoons table salt

1 teaspoon freshly milled pepper

6 large soft hamburger buns

6 thick slices large red-ripe tomatoes (skip them rather than use poor quality)

Crisp iceberg lettuce leaves (no microgreens here)

Slices of mild onion, dill pickle slices, spoonfuls of pickle relish, crisply cooked bacon slices, optional

Fire up the grill for a two-level fire capable of cooking first on high heat (1 to 2 seconds with the hand test) and then on medium heat (4 to 5 seconds with the hand test).

Combine the mayonnaise and ketchup in a small bowl and reserve.

Mix together the ground chuck, salt, and pepper. Gently form the mixture into six patties ½ to ¾ inch thick. The patties should hold together firmly, but avoid compacting them or handling them any longer than necessary.

Grill the burgers uncovered over high heat for 1 minute per side. Move the burgers to medium heat and rotate a half-turn for crisscross grill

marks. Cook for 4 to 5 minutes more per side for medium, until crusty and richly brown with a bare hint of pink at the center. Do not mash the burgers with the spatula, which only expels the savory juices. Toast the buns at the edge of the grill if you wish. Lay the burgers side by side on a platter after preparation rather than on top of one another.

Spoon the mayonnaise-ketchup mixture generously on both sides of a bun. Add the burger, tomato, lettuce, and any optional toppings, and repeat with the remaining burgers and ingredients. Eat the burgers hot from the grill, squeezing the buns gently to mingle all the juices.

Adding a Personal Signature:

Cheeseburgers are the natural next step up in heft. The common cheddar or Jack topping works well, and even those bland slices of so called American cheese taste acceptable. But break out of the box sometimes, adding a little more pungency with a cheese in the blue family, or maybe a brick cheese, or an extra-sharp cheddar. Whichever cheese you choose, leave it out for a while at room temperature so that it doesn't sit like a gold bar on top of the burgers. Lay it over the burgers right after you turn them upward for the last time.

Like all New Mexicans, we love green chile–cheeseburgers. Blacken and blister some mild long green chiles (sometimes called Anaheims) over medium to high heat on your grill, steam briefly in a plastic bag, strip off the skin, and chop the chiles. Spoon onto the bottom halves of the buns before adding the burgers. Use a mild cheese such as cheddar, Jack, or asadero.

Take a cue from California's commendable chain called Fatburger, "The Last Great Hamburger Stand," and top your meat with a fried egg.

ROSEMARY AND MINT LAMB BURGERS

In a blind tasting, many burger fans find that they like lamb burgers better than hamburgers. The meat is earthier, somehow more soulful, than beef, particularly when it's fresh, pasture-grazed lamb that hasn't been shipped frozen from halfway around the world. Ask for a shoulder cut, and as with beef, ask your butcher to grind it if you will be grilling it within a few hours, or else bring it home to chop in your food processor just before making the burgers. Pre-ground lamb in the meat case often comes from particularly fatty sections of the lamb, so it's likely to cause more flare-ups when grilling.

Serves 6

2 pounds freshly ground lamb shoulder

½ cup minced fresh mint

3 tablespoons finely minced fresh rosemary or 1½ tablespoons finely crumbled dried rosemary, lightly packed

1 to 1½ teaspoons coarse salt, either kosher or sea salt

12 slices sourdough bread

Mayonnaise

Fire up the grill, bringing the temperature to medium (4 to 5 seconds with the hand test).

In a medium bowl, mix together the ground lamb, mint, rosemary, and salt. Gently form the mixture into 4 patties about ½ to ¾ inch thick. The patties should hold together firmly, but don't compact them or handle them any more than necessary.

Grill the burgers uncovered over medium heat for a total of 5 to 5½ minutes per side for medium-rare. Rotate a half-turn, halfway through cooking on each side, for crisscross grill marks. Toast the bread at the edge of the grill if you wish.

Serve each burger between two slices of sourdough, slathered with mayonnaise.

Adding a Personal Signature:

If you want to add cheese, try feta cheese crumbled over the burgers near the end of cooking.

Curry goes great with lamb in many dishes, including burgers. One approach is to substitute a couple of teaspoons of curry powder for the rosemary. Another is to create a tasty topping to put on the hot burgers by stirring together ¾ cup sour cream, ¾ cup mayonnaise, ¼ cup plus 2 tablespoons mango chutney, and at least 1 tablespoon of curry powder. Personally, we'd do both.

MOROCCAN PICNIC SUPPER

Store-bought hummus with pita triangles

Rosemary and Mint Lamb Burgers

Moroccan Carrot Salad (page 162)

Berry Right-Side-Up Cake (page 171)

Mint iced tea

TURKEY BURGERS

We eat these because they taste great, not because of presumed health benefits. As with beef and lamb, it's best for the turkey to be freshly ground, by you or your market. Use thigh meat for maximum flavor, mixed with a little Worcestershire sauce and mustard, then covered with a dry spice rub. If you need to make a substitution, choose chicken thighs over turkey breast meat. Like lamb burgers, turkey patties grill best over a steady medium flame, but unlike other burgers, they should be cooked almost well-done.

Serves 6

½ cup mayonnaise

2 to 3 tablespoons Dijon mustard

DRY RUB

1 tablespoon plus 1 teaspoon crumbled dried thyme

2 teaspoons crumbled dried sage

2 teaspoons freshly milled black pepper

1½ teaspoons kosher salt

1 teaspoon ground white pepper

2 pounds freshly ground boneless turkey thighs

2 teaspoons Dijon mustard

2 teaspoons Worcestershire sauce

6 onion rolls, split, or hamburger buns, preferably bakery-made (not supermarket)

Lettuce leaves or shredded red cabbage

Fire up the grill, bringing the temperature to medium (4 to 5 seconds with the hand test).

Combine the mayonnaise and mustard in a small bowl and reserve.

Prepare the burgers, first stirring together the dry rub ingredients. Combine the ground turkey, mustard, and Worcestershire. Gently form the mixture into six patties about ½ inch thick. The patties should hold together firmly, but don't compact them or handle them any more than necessary. The meat tends to be soft, and if it becomes too soft to form, return it to the refrigerator or freezer briefly. Sprinkle the rub over both sides of the burgers evenly.

Grill the burgers uncovered over medium heat for about 8 to 9 minutes per side, until medium-brown and crispy with a fully cooked interior, 165°F on an instant-read thermometer inserted into a burger from its side. Rotate a half-turn, halfway through cooking on each side, for crisscross grill marks. Toast the rolls at the edge of the grill if you wish.

Spread the mayonnaise mixture on both sides of the rolls, add lettuce leaves, and top with the burgers. Serve immediately.

Adding a Personal Signature:

If turkey makes you think of Thanksgiving, go with the notion, replacing the mayo-mustard with cranberry chutney.

TUNA BURGERS

Tuna steaks make super burgers, more "uptown" than their peers and every bit as tasty. Because you're working with fairly thin steaks, start with them cold, to make sure they aren't overcooked in the center before the surface is nicely colored.

Serves 4

WASABI-SCALLION MAYONNAISE

½ cup mayonnaise

2 scallions, roots and limp tops trimmed, minced

1 teaspoon wasabi paste, or more to taste

1 tablespoons teriyaki sauce

2 teaspoons toasted sesame oil

Two 1-inch-thick tuna steaks, approximately 12 ounces each, cut horizontally in half to create four ½-inch-thick steaks, chilled

Coarse salt, either kosher or sea salt

8 slices good white bread

Crisp watercress, butter lettuce leaves, or shredded romaine

MENU FOR A
TERRIFIC PACIFIC
SUNDAY LUNCH

Asian Appetizer Platter (page 42)

Tuna Burgers

Piña Colada Sorbet (page 172)

Shortbread cookies

Prepare the mayonnaise, combining the ingredients in a small bowl. Reserve.

Fire up the grill, bringing the temperature to medium-high (3 seconds with the hand test).

Stir together the teriyaki sauce and oil, and coat the steaks very lightly with the mixture. Sprinkle lightly with salt.

Transfer the steaks to a well-oiled grate. Grill for 2 to 3 minutes per side, until lightly browned with a touch of pink at the very center. Toast the bread at the edge of the grill if you wish.

Spread mayonnaise on the bread slices. Top half with the tuna steaks and watercress. Crown with remaining bread slices. Serve hot.

A Passion for Tenderloin

Aside from salmon and maybe steaks, nothing is more popular on up-scale restaurant menus these days than pork tenderloin. Everyone seems to love the leanness, the tenderness, and the affordability. Even more important to us personally, tenderloin welcomes a wide range of flavoring, perhaps more than any other high-quality meat.

Compared to other pork cuts, it also grills well. Today's lean pork chops dry out easily even on moderate heat, and ribs require more time and attention than many cooks can give. Like a fine steak, start tenderloins over a hot fire, sear their surface thoroughly, and then move them to medium heat to cook through. To keep them succulent, avoid cooking tenderloins beyond an internal temperature of 155°F to 160°F, when the centers are just barely white and the juices run clear. If your tenderloins turn out to be larger than the size suggested in a recipe, grill them a little longer than specified over the medium fire. In all cases, check for doneness with an instant-read meat thermometer. As long as you don't overcook them, tenderloins will repay your passion in munificent ways.

CLASSIC CRUSTY PORK TENDERLOIN

Dry spice rubs mate beautifully with pork tenderloins, particularly rubs with a hint of sugar to help caramelize and crust the surface. Most meat markets package tenderloins in pairs. Even if you don't intend to finish both in one meal, consider cooking them together because the cold pork tastes great the next day, simply sliced and plated or piled on a sandwich.

Serves 6

DRY RUB

2 tablespoons espresso powder	1 teaspoon freshly milled pepper
1 tablespoon turbinado sugar ("Sugar in the Raw")	
2 teaspoons ground dried chipotle chile	Two 12- to 14-ounce sections of pork tenderloin
2 teaspoons coarse salt, either kosher or sea salt	

Stir together the dry rub ingredients in a small bowl. Massage the mixture into the tenderloins and let sit covered at room temperature for 20 to 30 minutes.

Fire up the grill for a two-level fire capable of cooking first on high heat (1 to 2 seconds with the hand test) and then on medium (4 to 5 seconds with the hand test).

Arrange the tenderloins on the grill over high heat, angling their thinner ends away from the hottest part of the fire. Grill uncovered for 5 minutes, rolling them on all sides. Move the tenderloin to medium heat and estimate the rest of the cooking time by the thickness of the meat. Skinny tenderloins (about 1½ inches in diameter) require an additional 8 to 10 minutes over medium heat. Plump tenderloins (up to 2½ inches in diameter) may need twice that long. Continue rolling on all sides for even cooking and a fully crusted surface. The pork is ready when its internal temperature reaches 155°F to 160°F. Let it rest for 5 minutes, covered with foil, before carving. We think very thin slices offer the best flavor, but cut it whatever way pleases you.

Adding a Personal Signature:

Create your own dry rub for pork tenderloin, mixing and matching ingredients such as those in the recipe with other complementary flavors.

- Sweet paprika, chili powder, coarse salt, cumin, and brown sugar or granulated sugar in the same proportions as the main dry rub

- 2 heaping teaspoons ground allspice, $1\frac{1}{2}$ teaspoons turbinado sugar or $\frac{3}{4}$ teaspoon granulated sugar, 1 heaping teaspoon coarse salt, $\frac{3}{4}$ teaspoon ground cinnamon, $\frac{1}{2}$ teaspoon ground white pepper

- 2 tablespoons whole black peppercorns, 1 tablespoon whole white peppercorns, 1 tablespoon whole pink peppercorns, 1 tablespoon coarse salt, $\frac{3}{4}$ teaspoon yellow mustard seeds, mixed and ground coarsely in a blender or spice mill, or placed in a plastic bag and cracked coarsely with a mallet

- 1 tablespoon crumbled dried marjoram or oregano, 1 tablespoon grated lemon zest, $1\frac{1}{2}$ teaspoons coarse salt, 1 teaspoon ground cumin, and $\frac{1}{2}$ teaspoon freshly milled pepper.

BUTTERFLIED THAI PORK TENDERLOIN

Slice open each tenderloin like a book to double the impact of this bold Thai-style marinade. The marinade caramelizes on the exposed surface over the fire, creating a delectable crunch as you bite into each succulent slice. Serve with or over a salad of soft-textured greens with a generous handful each of fresh mint, basil, and cilantro.

Serves 6

MARINADE

¼ cup soy sauce

¼ cup Asian fish sauce

¼ cup packed brown sugar, preferably dark brown

2 tablespoons thawed pineapple juice concentrate or ¼ cup pineapple juice

2 tablespoons fresh lime juice (about 1 medium lime)

2 tablespoons chopped fresh ginger

1 teaspoon five-spice powder or 1 star anise, crushed

1 teaspoon crushed dried hot red chile, or Asian chile paste

Two 12- to 14-ounce sections of pork tenderloin, butterflied lengthwise and pounded to ¾-inch thickness

Stir together the marinade ingredients in a small bowl. Place the tenderloins in a large zippered plastic bag. Pour the marinade over them, seal, and toss back and forth to coat the tenderloins evenly. Let sit at room temperature for 20 to 30 minutes.

Fire up the grill for a two-level fire capable of cooking first on high heat (1 to 2 seconds with the hand test) and then on medium (4 to 5 seconds with the hand test).

Drain the tenderloins, discarding the marinade. Leave in place any spices that cling to the surface.

Arrange the tenderloins flat on the grill with their thinner ends angled away from the hottest part of the fire. Grill over high heat for 4 minutes, turning once. Move the tenderloins to medium heat and continue cooking for 8 to 10 more minutes. Turn at least 2 more times for even cooking, more often if juices begin to pool on the surface. The pork is done when its internal temperature reaches 155°F to 160°F. Let it rest for 5 minutes, covered with foil, before carving.

Adding a Personal Signature:

Thai pork makes a great Asian-style sandwich, in the Vietnamese tradition of *bahn mi*. Start with a section of a split French baguette and smear with mayonnaise. If you wish, add a sprinkle of Asian chile sauce or fish sauce to the mayo. Top with pork, and then some vinegar marinated cucumber slices, some shredded carrot or a few jalapeño slices, and a good sprinkling of cilantro.

STUFFED TENDERLOIN WITH FIGS, BACON, AND CHARRED ONIONS

Double up a pair of tenderloins for this party dish. You butterfly each, sandwich a lusty filling between the two, secure them like a pretty present, and rub with a cracked pepper mixture.

Serves 8

FILLING

1 medium onion, sliced ⅓ inch thick

Vegetable oil spray

¼ pound uncooked bacon, chopped

2 tablespoons butter

1 cup chopped dried figs (about 6 ounces)

2 tablespoons red wine vinegar or fig vinegar

¾ cup dry coarse bread crumbs

Approximately ½ cup chicken stock or water

Two 12- to 14-ounce sections of pork tenderloin, butterflied lengthwise and pounded to ½-inch thickness

DRY RUB

1 tablespoon freshly cracked pepper

1 teaspoon turbinado sugar ("Sugar in the Raw") or brown sugar

1 teaspoon coarse salt, either kosher or sea salt

BASTE

2 tablespoons butter

2 tablespoons chicken stock or water

2 teaspoons red wine vinegar or fig vinegar

Fire up the grill for a two-level fire capable of cooking on high heat (1 to 2 seconds with the hand test) and on medium (4 to 5 seconds with the hand test).

Run a toothpick through each onion slice to hold the rings together, then spray lightly with oil.

Grill the onion slices over medium heat until nearly tender with some charred edges, 8 to 10 minutes. Remove the onion slices and when cool enough to handle chop them coarsely. Warm a skillet over the grill's medium heat (or over a kitchen burner if you prefer). Fry the bacon in the skillet until brown and beginning to crisp. Remove the bacon with a slotted spoon and drain it. Add the butter to the drippings and when melted, stir in the onion and figs. Cook several more minutes until the onion is soft, then stir in the vinegar, bread crumbs, and bacon. Remove from the heat and stir in enough stock to make the mixture moist. It should hold together easily, but not get soupy.

Trim the tenderloins to equal size. Spoon the filling evenly over one tenderloin, almost to the edges. Top with the second open tenderloin. With several lengths of kitchen string, tie the pork package up neatly. We go around the tenderloins lengthwise twice, and then turn and crisscross the string a half-dozen times around their girth. Spray all over with vegetable oil. The whole package should be about 2 inches thick throughout. Stir together the dry rub (pepper, sugar, and salt) and rub it over all sides.

Warm the baste in a small container at the edge of the grill, melting the butter. Reserve.

Transfer the stuffed tenderloin to the grill, arranging it first over high heat. Grill for about 3 minutes per side. Roll the pork over to medium heat and continue to grill for 18 to 22 more minutes. Roll over several times and brush lightly each time with the baste. The pork is ready when its internal temperature reaches 155°F to 160°F. If, after 22 minutes over medium heat, the pork is not getting close to 155°F, the meat may be thicker than optimum or the grill may be losing heat over time. Cover the grill if needed, for a few more minutes of cooking, until done.

Let the pork rest for 5 minutes, covered with foil, before carving. Snip off the string. Cut in inch-thick slices down through the filling and both layers of meat. Transfer carefully to plates so that the filling stays sandwiched between the layers of tenderloin. Enjoy.

Adding a Personal Signature:

Dress up the filling in a personal way, possibly:

- Stir a few tablespoons of port, Armagnac, or brandy into the filling before it's cooked down

- add about ¼ cup of any crumbled blue cheese to the filling at the same time as the bread crumbs

- substitute dates for the figs or pancetta for the bacon

FATHER'S DAY CELEBRATION

Crisp romaine hearts with blue cheese dressing

Stuffed Tenderloin with Figs, Bacon, and Charred Onions

Warm Potato Salad (page 163)

Buttered corn on the cob

S'mores made with chocolate mints

PRIMO CUBANO SANDWICHES

The Cuban sandwich, or *medianoche*, has gained popularity throughout the United States, but many commercial versions don't really cut the mustard. You can do better at home, where the pork, cheese, and pickle combo makes superb fare for a casual party. For authenticity and taste both, we like to toast the sandwiches in a sandwich press or waffle iron, to melt the cheese and crust the bread. Many standard waffle irons have reversible cooking plates that can be turned to a smooth side perfect for providing the desired heat and heavy surface. If you don't have a press or a waffle iron, simply warm the filled sandwiches over a low grill fire.

Serve 6

MOJO

One 6-ounce can frozen orange juice concentrate, thawed

Juice of 3 key limes or 2 regular limes (3 to 4 tablespoons)

¼ cup olive oil

3 plump garlic cloves, chopped

1 tablespoon minced fresh oregano or 1½ teaspoons dried oregano or marjoram

1 teaspoon coarse salt, either kosher or sea salt, or 1½ teaspoons store-bought adobo seasoning

Several splashes of Caribbean-style habanero hot sauce, optional

1 to 1¼ pound pork tenderloin

2 tablespoons prepared yellow mustard

6 French rolls or Cuban rolls or bread

Dill pickle slices, enough to cover each sandwich

12 thin slices ham

12 thin slices Swiss cheese

Whisk together the mojo ingredients. Set aside ¼ cup plus 2 tablespoons of the mojo. Place the tenderloin in a zippered plastic bag and pour the rest of the mojo over it. Toss back and forth to cover the pork and set aside at room temperature for 30 minutes (or refrigerate for up to several hours, and then let sit at room temperature for 20 to 30 minutes before proceeding).

Fire up the grill for a two-level fire capable of cooking first on high heat (1 to 2 seconds with the hand test) and then on medium heat (4 to 5 seconds with the hand test).

Arrange the tenderloin on the grill over high heat with the thin tail end angled away from the hottest part of the fire. Grill the tenderloin over high heat for 5 minutes, rolling it on all sides. Move the tenderloin to medium heat and estimate the rest of the cooking time by the thickness of the meat. Skinny tenderloins (about 1½ inches in diameter) require an additional 8 to 10 minutes over medium heat. Plump tenderloins (up to 2½ inches in diameter) may need twice that long. Continue rolling the meat occasionally to cook evenly. The pork is done when its internal temperature reaches 155°F to 160°F. Let it rest, covered with foil, for 5 minutes, then slice thinly.

Mix the reserved mojo with mustard. If the rolls are very thick and bready, tear out some of the center bread and discard it. Slather both sides of a bun with mojo mustard. Layer pickles generously across the bottom, add 2 ham slices, then a munificent layer of pork tenderloin and 2 cheese slices. Cap with the top half of the roll, and repeat for remaining sandwiches. Toast each sandwich at the edge of the grill or—even better—in a sandwich press or waffle iron until lightly brown and crisp. Serve immediately.

CARIBBEAN PARTY

Jicama slices sprinkled with lime juice and dried mild red chile

Primo Cubano Sandwiches

Sweet potato chips

Passionate Mangos (page 152)

Caribbean Rum Punch (page 178)

PORK TENDERLOIN MEDALLIONS WITH LEMON-MUSTARD SAUCE

Medallions—thick disks of tenderloin—make a stylish presentation for meat, especially if they sit in a pool of sauce so tasty that you'll dab it up with the handiest chunk of bread.

Serves 6

Two 12- to 14-ounce sections of pork tenderloin

MUSTARD RUB

2 tablespoons Dijon mustard

2 teaspoons coarsely ground pepper

2 teaspoons brown sugar

2 teaspoons coarse salt, either kosher or sea salt

1 teaspoon vegetable oil

LEMON-MUSTARD SAUCE

¼ cup butter, preferably unsalted

¼ cup minced shallots

1 cup chicken stock

1 teaspoon Dijon mustard

2 tablespoons fresh lemon juice

2 teaspoons minced parsley, preferably flat-leaf, optional

Coarse salt, either kosher or sea salt

Cut off any scrawny tail ends from the tenderloins. Slice each tenderloin into 6 equal rounds. Pound the medallions lightly with a meat mallet or rolling pin to one inch in thickness. Mix together the mustard rub ingredients. Coat the medallions with the rub. Let sit uncovered at room temperature while the grill heats.

Fire up the grill for a two-level fire capable of cooking first on high heat (1 to 2 seconds with the hand test) and then on medium heat (4 to 5 seconds with the hand test)

Make the sauce, first melting the butter in a skillet over medium heat. Add the shallots and cook until soft and beginning to color, about 5 minutes. Stir in the chicken stock and mustard, and continue cooking until reduced by about one half. Stir in the lemon juice, parsley, and salt to taste. Keep the sauce warm.

Transfer the pork medallions to the grill over high heat. Grill for about 2 minutes per side. Move to medium heat, rotating the medallions a half-turn for crisscross grill marks. Continue cooking for 3 to 4 minutes more per side, until the medallions' internal temperature reaches 155°F to 160°F. If any of the medallions begins to look dry, drizzle a bit of the sauce over it. Pool the sauce on individual plates and serve 1 or 2 medallions to a portion.

Chicken, Turkey, Rotisserie and Lamb

When people cooked with a wood fire in kitchen hearths, they often spit-roasted poultry and meat on a rotisserie positioned at the front of the fireplace and the flame. The method yields better results than modern oven roasting, basting foods in their natural fats while crisping the surface and retaining internal succulence. The live fire and revolving spit produce a dinner that's literally "done to a turn."

Rotisserie roasting is enjoying a major resurgence. An increasing number of grills, particularly new gas models, feature a motorized spit placed in front of the cooking fire rather than above it. Among all the frills offered with grills today, this is the only one that really excites us. For whole birds and cuts of meat too large to grill over a direct flame, it provides a perfect alternative to grilling, giving results just as crisp and juicy. The cooking method dazzles friends and so does the food, making rotisserie roasting ideal for an outdoor party. Take a turn at it and you'll never turn back.

HERB-ROASTED ROTISSERIE CHICKEN

Nothing rivals spit-roasting in front of the fire as a way of cooking a whole chicken—producing lusciously juicy, golden-crisp birds—but few grill manufacturers provide adequate instructions on how to do it well. That's also true of directions that come with rotisseries designed to cook above the fire, such as optional attachments for charcoal grills and pared-down or older gas models. Here's our blueprint for success with both kinds of rotisseries. The directions are detailed because the process is new to many people. By the second time, you'll probably only glance at the fine print, and by the third time, we'll wager that you'll be flying solo. To serve more than four people, get more chickens of the same size and cook multiple birds simultaneously.

Serves 2 to 4 or more

1 or more plump whole chickens, 3¼ to 3½ pounds each

Coarse salt, either kosher or sea salt

Freshly milled pepper

Butter, olive oil, goose fat, duck fat, or other flavorful fat, optional

Fresh minced herbs and sprigs, such as tarragon, rosemary, basil or thyme

1 lemon or small orange, cut into wedges

At least one hour and up to a day before you plan to roast the chicken, season the chicken. If your rotisserie cooks in front of the flame rather than above it, and you want to use the fat for extra flavor, rub it on the chicken at the same time. Don't use the fat if you're cooking above the flame because much of it will drip away and increase flare-ups. Loosen the skin all over, gently nudging your fingers down under it, including the skin on the drumsticks. Rub the chicken generously with the salt, pepper, butter, and minced herbs under and over the skin, being careful to avoid tearing the skin.

After rubbing, place a few herb sprigs or citrus sections into the chicken's body cavity. Place the chicken in a large zippered plastic bag, seal, and refrigerate. Let sit at room temperature about 20 minutes before proceeding.

Truss the chicken, which ensures even cooking and keeps the bird from flopping around on the spit. Cut a piece of kitchen twine about four feet

long. Set the chicken breast up on a work surface. Starting in the middle of your piece of string, wrap it around the ends of both legs, then crisscross the string back and forth around the chicken up to the neck end. Pay special attention to the wings, since you want the wings flush against the chicken's body. Tie the string ends together when you have wrapped the rest around the bird.

Fire up the rotisserie, removing the spit first if it's in place, and heat the grill with the lid closed. Use the set rotisserie temperature, if your grill functions that way, or bring the heat to medium (4 to 5 seconds with the hand test).

Slide one of the prongs onto the far end of the spit, facing toward the center. Next slide on the chicken, legs first, running the spit through the cavity. Secure the legs to the prong. Slide on the second prong and attach it to the chicken's neck end. (If you are adding a second chicken, or more, you will need a center prong piece that juts in both directions, or another pair of prongs, for each additional bird.)

Position the chicken in the center of the spit, and tighten the bolts on the prongs. If your rotisserie has a counterweight that fits on the spit or its handle, secure it in place. Attach the spit to the motor and turn on the power.

Close the grill cover unless the manufacturer's instructions say otherwise. Cook 70 to 90 minutes depending on the type of rotisserie, until an instant-read thermometer stuck in the thickest part of a thigh reads 170°F to 175°F. Don't open the cover too often or you will increase the cooking time substantially.

With heatproof mitts, remove the spit from the grill. Unscrew the counterweight and bolts, and slide off the chicken and prongs. Rest the chicken on a large cutting board. Pull off the prongs and snip off the twine. Let it sit about 10 minutes, so the juices can settle, then carve and serve.

Adding a Personal Signature:

Nearly any sauce can accompany a simply seasoned rotisserie chicken. Just serve it on the side to avoid drowning the crisp skin. We call a quick favorite Red Hot and Orange Sauce, combining a tomato-based barbecue sauce and thawed frozen orange juice concentrate in about equal proportions along with a few good splashes of Tabasco sauce or the smokier Tabasco chipotle sauce.

Every local open-air market in France includes at least one rotisserie chicken vendor cooking his fare on-site. Do as he does, arranging chunks of potatoes, carrots, onions, parsnips, and other roasting vegetables under the chicken so that they cook in the scrumptious drippings. Cut the vegetables in roughly equal 1-inch cubes, put them in a foil-lined pan, stir once or twice as they cook, and they'll be done at the same time as the bird.

LABOR DAY PARTY

BLT Salad with Warm Bacon Dressing (page 158)

Herb-Roasted Rotisserie Chicken

Corn Pudding (page 166)

Melon with Sparkling Wine (page 168)

SPIT-ROASTED TURKEY BREAST

A whole turkey, cooked to a turn, makes the ultimate in Thanksgiving grandeur, but it's not exactly casual party food. A turkey breast offers equally fine eating with a much smaller investment in time and logistics, making it a better option for an outdoor gathering of friends. Like the previous chicken, this is the basic preparation, very tasty as is but open to signature seasonings. The only tricky part is getting the spit pushed down through the breast, which may require an ice pick or other pointed tool to get the job underway. If you plan to rotiss turkey breast frequently, or other meats without a natural cavity, look for a cage- or cradle-style replacement for the standard spit to avoid the need to force the shaft through the breast. E-Z Cue (877-377-2900) is one source.

Serves 8 or more	
1 bone-in, skin-on turkey breast, 4½ to 5½ pounds	Butter, olive oil, goose fat, duck fat, or other flavorful fat, optional
Coarse salt, either kosher or sea salt, and freshly milled pepper, or a favorite dry rub	Fresh herb sprigs, optional

At least one hour and up to a day before you plan to roast the turkey breast, season it. If your rotisserie cooks in front of the flame rather than above it, and you want to use the fat for extra flavor, rub it on the turkey breast at the same time. Don't use the fat if you're cooking above the flame because much of it will drip away and increase flare-ups. Loosen the skin all over, gently nudging your fingers down under it. Rub the turkey breast generously with the salt and pepper or dry rub, under and over the skin, being careful to avoid tearing the skin. If using the herbs, nudge them under the skin as well.

Place the turkey breast in a large zippered plastic bag, seal, and refrigerate until about 20 minutes before you plan to cook. Let it sit at room temperature before proceeding.

Fire up the rotisserie, removing the spit first if it's in place, and heat the grill with the lid closed. Use the set rotisserie temperature, if your grill functions that way, or bring the heat to medium (4 to 5 seconds with the hand test).

Slide one of the prongs onto the far end of the spit, facing toward the center. Next slide on the turkey breast, with what would have been its head end first. In order to distribute the weight evenly, run the spit halfway between the wings, but about 1 inch closer to the front of the breast than the back. If your spit end isn't fairly sharp, you may need to poke a hole down through the breast with an ice pick, pair of kitchen scissors, or a sharp, sturdy metal skewer. Secure the breast to the prong. Slide on the second prong and attach it to the other, smaller end.

Position the turkey breast in the center of the spit, and tighten the bolts on the prongs. If your rotisserie has a counterweight that fits on the spit or its handle, secure it in place. Attach the spit to the motor and turn on the power.

Close the grill cover unless the manufacturer's instructions say otherwise. Cook 1½ to 2 hours depending on the size of the breast and type of rotisserie, until an instant-read thermometer stuck in the thickest part of the breast reads 165°F to 170°F. Don't open the cover too often or you will increase the cooking time substantially.

With heatproof mitts, remove the spit from the grill. Unscrew the counterweight and bolts, and slide the turkey breast and prongs off. Rest the turkey breast on a large cutting board. Pull off the prongs. Let it sit about 10 minutes, so the juices can settle, then carve and serve.

Adding a Personal Signature:

Flavoring pastes, which are wet versions of the dry rub, work great with turkey breasts. Just slather the paste on an hour or two before you begin cooking. For starters try these, each of which should be pureed in a blender or food processor:

- ½ cup packed fresh thyme leaves, ½ cup fresh parsley leaves, 4 garlic cloves, 2 teaspoons coarse salt, and ½ cup olive oil

- 3.5-ounce package Mexican achiote paste, 2 garlic cloves, ⅓ cup orange juice, and 1 tablespoon lime juice

SPANISH LEG OF LAMB

We once enjoyed a magnificent meal in the village of Haro, deep in Spain's Rioja wine country, at a simple restaurant that specializes exclusively in lamb haunches expertly roasted in a wood-burning fireplace. Back home, we used the experience as the inspiration for this rotisserie-roasted leg of lamb.

Serves 8

MARINADE

½ cup flavorful olive oil

½ cup dry sherry

½ cup minced fresh tarragon

8 to 10 plump garlic cloves, slivered

1 tablespoon coarse salt, either kosher or sea salt

5- to 5½-pound boned and tied leg of lamb

GREEN OLIVE SAUCE

1 cup pitted green olives with character, with 1 to 2 tablespoons brine (we prefer Spanish olives marinated with garlic)

½ cup flavorful olive oil

1 to 2 tablespoons minced fresh tarragon, optional

At least one hour and up to a day before you plan to roast the leg of lamb, combine the marinade ingredients. Place the lamb in a large plastic bag or in a large shallow dish. Pour the marinade over the lamb and use your hands to rub some of the marinade (especially the garlic slices) into the meat's crevices. Seal and refrigerate until about 30 minutes before you plan to cook, turning the meat occasionally. Drain and discard the marinade, and let the lamb sit uncovered at room temperature. Pat the surface dry.

Prepare the olive sauce, pureeing the ingredients in a blender or food processor. Let sit at room temperature.

Fire up the rotisserie, removing the spit first if it's in place, and heat the grill with the lid closed. Use the set rotisserie temperature, if your grill functions that way, or bring the heat to medium (4 to 5 seconds with the hand test).

Slide one of the prongs onto the far end of the spit, facing toward the center. Next slide on the lamb, running the spit through the center, working it through the meat. Secure the first end to the prong. Slide on the second prong and attach it to the other end of the meat.

Position the lamb in the center of the spit, and tighten the bolts on the prongs. If your rotisserie has a counterweight that fits on the spit or its handle, secure it in place. Attach the spit to the motor and turn on the power.

Close the grill cover unless the manufacturer's instructions say otherwise. Cook 45 to 60 minutes depending on the mass of the lamb and the type of rotisserie, until well browned and medium-rare, when an instant-read thermometer reads 125°F to 130°F. Baste once with the drippings after about 30 minutes. Don't open the cover too often or you will increase the cooking time substantially.

With heatproof mitts, remove the spit from the grill. Unscrew the counterweight and bolts, and slide off the lamb and prongs. Rest the lamb on a large cutting board. Pull off the prongs and snip off the twine or netting. Let it sit about 10 minutes, so the juices can settle, then carve into thin slices. Give the sauce a stir and serve it immediately with the lamb.

SPLENDID EASTER
DINNER

**Goat Cheese Wrapped in Grape
Leaves (page 15)**

Spanish Leg of Lamb

**Your choice of the Great Green Salads
(page 165)**

Fresh peas with mint

Lemon meringue pie

Quick Chick

Savvy grillers serve chicken a lot when they're cooking for a small crowd. Everyone enjoys chicken, at least when it's grilled well, and unlike many foods, few people balk at it for health or dietary reasons. Boneless, skinless breasts—easily the most popular part for grilling—also cook in a snap and welcome a whole world of seasoning. They make ideal party fare, ready to dance to any tune you want to play.

The only potential hitch is grilling the breasts properly to get a lightly browned, crispy surface and a tender, juicy center. Thousands of grillers regularly cook them on a fire that's too hot for their fair flesh, charring the outside and leaving them raw inside, or they leave the breasts over the heat too long, turning them as dry as hay. To avoid those pitfalls, pound breasts to an even thickness, so they cook uniformly, and grill with a steady medium heat. Measure the fire carefully with the hand test (page 7) before you put the chicken on the grate, and maintain that temperature until the end, tracking the time as you grill. With those simple steps, you'll always succeed as a cook, and when you do, your party will always succeed as well.

TANGY THAI CHICKEN

Simple to make, with easily found ingredients, but exotic and complex in taste—that's the beauty of these breasts. Serve them with white rice or on mixed greens with a peanut oil vinaigrette.

Serves 4

1 tablespoon store-bought red or green Thai curry paste, or more to taste

2 teaspoons peanut oil or vegetable oil

One 15-ounce can coconut milk

Salt or Asian fish sauce, optional

4 medium to large boneless, skinless chicken breasts, pounded ½ inch thick

Store-bought sweet Thai red chile sauce

Chopped peanuts and chopped fresh mint, basil, or cilantro or a combination

Make the marinade, first combining the curry paste and oil in a bowl and stirring until the paste is softened. Mix in three quarters of the coconut milk and taste the mixture. If it tastes bland now, it will taste even blander on the chicken, so add more curry paste, and salt if needed, until the mixture is pleasantly pungent. If the mixture becomes too spicy, add a little more coconut milk. Place the chicken in a zippered plastic bag, pour the marinade over it, and seal the bag. Toss back and forth to coat the chicken evenly. Let sit at room temperature for 20 minutes while you prepare the grill. For a more intense flavor, marinate for up to several hours, refrigerated.

Fire up the grill, bringing the heat to medium (4 to 5 seconds with the hand test).

Drain the chicken, discarding the marinade. Grill the chicken for 10 to 12 minutes total. Turn onto each side twice, rotating the breasts a half-turn each time for crisscross grill marks.

After each side of the chicken has faced the fire once, brush them with a few tablespoons of the chile sauce. The chicken is ready when it is white throughout but still juicy and the surface is a bit chewy and caramelized in spots.

The breasts can be served whole or thickly sliced and mounded on a platter. Sprinkle with chopped peanuts or herbs or both, and accompany with additional sweet chile sauce.

Adding a Personal Signature:

Turn from Thailand to India for inspiration. Replace the coconut milk with about 1 cup of plain yogurt and replace the curry paste with good fresh curry powder or garam masala. Skip the chile sauce glaze, but do sprinkle with cilantro before serving.

Use the chicken as a filling for summer rolls. Dampen Asian rice paper wrappers briefly in warm water and pat off excess water. Then roll up chicken shreds and all the garnishes into 1-inch-diameter cylinders with the ends tucked in (like a burrito). For dunking, serve with the sweet Thai red chile sauce or mix some of the sauce into about an equal amount of white vinegar.

ALL-AMERICAN BARBECUED CHICKEN BREASTS

This is the backyard classic, loved across the land, though we make it here with boneless, skinless breasts rather than the more traditional bone-in parts. Don't cop out and use a bottled barbecue sauce. It's the sauce that gives you a bragging-rights claim to the dish, so make your own.

Serves 4 or more

SAUCE

1 cup ketchup

¼ cup molasses

2 tablespoons brown sugar

2 tablespoons butter

1½ tablespoons Worcestershire sauce

2 teaspoons prepared yellow mustard

1 teaspoon onion powder

¼ teaspoon freshly milled pepper

¼ teaspoon chili powder

3 to 4 tablespoons bourbon

4 medium to large boneless, skinless chicken breasts, pounded ½ inch thick

½ cup Worcestershire sauce

2 teaspoons vegetable oil

½ teaspoon table salt

Prepare the sauce. Combine the ketchup, molasses, brown sugar, butter, 1½ tablespoons of Worcestershire, mustard, onion powder, pepper, and chili powder in a saucepan with ½ cup water and bring to a boil. Reduce the heat to a bare simmer and cook for 5 to 10 minutes until thickened lightly. Stir in the bourbon and simmer another couple of minutes. Remove from the heat and set aside about one half of the sauce to serve with the chicken at the table.

Place the chicken in a zippered plastic bag and pour the ½ cup of Worcestershire over it. Add the oil and salt, and seal the bag. Toss back and forth to coat the chicken evenly. Let sit for 20 to 30 minutes at room temperature.

Fire up the grill, bringing the heat to medium (4 to 5 seconds with the hand test).

Drain the chicken and discard the marinade. Pat any liquid standing on the surface with a paper towel.

Grill the chicken for 10 to 12 minutes total. Turn onto each side twice, rotating the breasts a half-turn each time for crisscross grill marks. After each side of the chicken has faced the fire once, begin brushing the sauce over the breasts. The chicken is ready when it is white throughout but still juicy and the surface is a bit chewy and caramelized in spots. If you wish, leave the chicken on the grill an extra minute or two to get a slightly crusty surface.

The breasts can be served whole or thickly sliced and mounded on a platter. Pass the remaining sauce on the side.

Adding a Personal Signature:

While a tomato-based barbecue sauce is the most typical type for this dish, experiment with other styles of barbecue sauce popular in various regions:

- equal amounts of prepared yellow mustard, white vinegar, and butter, melted together

- tangy vinegar sauce with 1 cup cider or white vinegar, 1 tablespoon sugar, 1 teaspoon salt, and ½ teaspoon freshly milled pepper or dried red chile flakes or both

- white sauce with 1 cup mayonnaise, 1 to 2 tablespoons cider vinegar, 1 tablespoon coarsely ground pepper, a few pinches of onion powder, and salt.

CHIPOTLE CHICKEN *SALPICÓN*

Salpicón means "hodgepodge" in Spanish, in this case an edible Mexican hodgepodge of a salad bursting with cubes of tender chicken and vegetables bound together with a mildly spicy dressing. It's a great way to use chicken that's been grilled ahead, giving you a chance to mingle and munch with your guests when they arrive.

Serves 6 or more

DRESSING/MARINADE

¼ cup plus 2 tablespoons vegetable oil

¼ cup fresh orange or tangerine juice

1 tablespoon fresh lime juice

1 minced canned chipotle chile with 1 tablespoon adobo sauce from the can, 2 tablespoons chipotle ketchup

1 garlic clove, minced

Salt

Freshly milled pepper

1 to 1¼ pounds boneless, skinless chicken breasts, pounded ½ inch thick

One 15-ounce can chickpeas, drained and rinsed

¼ pound mild cheese, such as Jack, asadero, or mild cheddar, diced chickpea-size

1 cucumber, peeled, seeded, and diced chickpea-size

1 small tomato, diced chickpea-size

½ small red onion, diced fine

1 ripe avocado, cubed

Cilantro leaves

Whisk together the dressing ingredients. Spoon 3 tablespoons of the dressing over the chicken, turning it once, then cover and let sit at room temperature while you get the grill going. Set the rest aside.

Fire up the grill, bringing the heat to medium (4 to 5 seconds with the hand test).

Grill the chicken uncovered over medium heat for 10 to 12 minutes total. Turn onto each side twice, rotating the breasts a half-turn each time for crisscross grill marks. The chicken is ready when white throughout but still juicy and the surface is a bit caramelized in spots.

Leave the chicken on the grill an extra minute or two, if you wish, to get a slightly crusty surface.

When cool enough to handle, cut the chicken into a neat dice, about the size of the chickpeas and vegetables. You want to be able to get a bit of everything in most bites. In a large bowl, toss together the chicken, chickpeas, cheese, cucumber, tomato, and onion with most of the dressing. (If you wish, the salpicón can be made ahead to this point and refrigerated up to overnight.) Add the avocado and, if you wish, more dressing, and combine gently. Spoon out onto a platter, scatter with cilantro, and serve.

Adding a Personal Signature:

Mix and match salad ingredients as you like. To us, the essential items are the chicken, avocado, and dressing. Everything else can come or go. Diced radish, celery, bell pepper, fresh chile, salad greens, summer squash, or zucchini could also be added to the toss-up or substituted for other vegetables.

HOISIN CHICKEN SALAD

Another fine salad, even better for a hot summer night because we serve the chicken chilled. Grill the breasts up to a day ahead, and then toss together the ingredients shortly before your friends are due.

Serves 4 or more as a main dish

4 medium to large boneless, skinless chicken breasts (1½ to 1¾ pounds), pounded ½ inch thick

Salt

HOISIN GLAZE

½ cup hoisin sauce

½ cup ketchup

¼ cup plus 2 tablespoons dry sherry, sake, or mirin (Japanese sweet rice wine)

Vegetable oil spray

3 tablespoons mayonnaise

1 tablespoon fresh lime juice

2 scallions, roots and limp tops trimmed, sliced thin on the diagonal

1 cup loosely packed slivered fresh juicy plums or peaches, or tangerine sections (membranes removed), or halved seedless grapes, or a combination

½ cup cilantro leaves

½ cup cashews or slivered almonds

½ cup wasabi-coated peas, cashews or slivered almonds, or chow mein noodles

Butter lettuce leaves, or other lettuce, optional

Salt the chicken, cover it, and let it sit for about 20 minutes.

Prepare the glaze, stirring together the ingredients in a small bowl. Add a bit of water if the mixture is too thick to brush easily.

Fire up the grill, bringing the heat to medium (4 to 5 seconds with the hand test).

Spray the chicken with vegetable oil. Grill the chicken for 10 to 12 minutes total. Turn onto each side twice, rotating the breasts a half-turn each time for crisscross grill marks. After each side of the chicken has faced the fire once, begin brushing the glaze over the breasts. The chicken is ready when it is white throughout but still juicy and the glaze is a bit chewy and caramelized in spots. If you wish, leave the chicken on the grill an extra minute or two to get a slightly crusty surface.

Chill the chicken at least 30 minutes or up to overnight. Slice it into neat cubes, ½- to ¾-inch square. Toss the chicken together with the mayonnaise, lime juice, scallions, and plums. Scatter the cilantro, cashews, and wasabi-coated peas over the salad, and serve on lettuce leaves if you wish.

CHICKEN WITH SAGE SANDWICH

We created a version of this sandwich for *Bon Appétit* magazine a few summers ago and liked it so much that we've continued to keep it on the front burner. It's a hit for parties because the combination of ingredients makes the sandwich out of the ordinary and gives it a touch of sophistication.

Serves 4 or more

SAGE PESTO

⅔ cup lightly packed fresh sage leaves

¼ cup lightly packed fresh Italian flat-leaf parsley leaves

1 plump garlic clove

½ cup pine nuts

¾ cup olive oil

¼ cup grated Parmesan or Pecorino Romano

Salt

Garlic-flavored olive oil or other olive oil

Salt

4 slices provolone

4 French rolls, split, or large sesame-seed buns

4 tablespoons mayonnaise

1 large Fuji apple, or other sweet, moderately-crisp variety

Sage sprigs, optional

4 medium boneless, skinless individual chicken breasts (approximately 1½ pounds), pounded ½ inch thick

Prepare the pesto in a food processor, first chopping together the sage, parsley, garlic, and pine nuts. With the machine running, drizzle in the oil in a thin steady stream. Add the cheese, and salt to taste, and process briefly to combine the mixture. Spoon into a bowl until ready to use. (Pesto can be made a day ahead, covered, and refrigerated. Let sit at room temperature for at least 15 minutes before serving.)

Rub the chicken breasts with just enough oil to coat them and sprinkle them lightly with salt. Cover the chicken and let it sit at room temperature for about 20 minutes while the grill heats.

Fire up the grill, bringing the temperature to medium (4 to 5 seconds with the hand test).

Grill the chicken over medium heat for 10 to 12 minutes total, turning onto each side twice, rotating the breasts a half-turn each time for crisscross grill marks. In the last couple of minutes of cooking, cover each breast with a cheese slice, cut to fit if necessary. The chicken is ready when white throughout but still juicy. Toast the rolls at the edge of the grill.

Coat the inside of the bottoms of the rolls generously with the mayonnaise. Core and slice the apples thin (about ⅛ inch) and arrange a layer of slices over the mayonnaise. Top each with a chicken breast. Spoon the pesto generously over the chicken. Cover the sandwich with the tops of the rolls. Sandwiches can be sliced into halves, if you wish, skewering each section together with toothpicks. Serve immediately, with optional sage sprigs on the side.

Sublime Shrimp

Serving shrimp conveys a message to friends that they're special people. Despite being the most popular shellfish in the country—relished by many folks who disdain seafood in general—shrimp still maintain an air of the exceptional and exclusive. They arrive at the table pretty and pink, looking like a little horn of plenty, and guests invariably devour them with delight.

With their distinctive taste, shrimp also can take on a wide range of assertive flavors without losing their own. Season them in your own style in advance or at the table. Be sure you really grill shrimp, though, instead of just steaming them on the grate in their shells. Peel them first, to apply direct heat to the surface, and cook them in a flash on a hot fire. The grilling takes little more than an instant but the pleasure of that moment lasts all night.

SHRIMP WITH LEMON CHIVE SAUCE

This simple, sunny preparation puts the spotlight on the flavor of the shrimp, bolstered slightly with the sparkle of lemon juice. We prefer to leave the shrimp tails on, but it's a matter of appearances rather than a rule.

Serves 4 or more

1½ pounds medium-large to large shrimp (about 30 per pound), peeled and, if you wish, deveined

1½ tablespoons olive oil

1 teaspoon coarse salt, either kosher or sea salt or more to taste

Freshly milled pepper

SAUCE

½ cup (1 stick) butter, preferably unsalted

2 tablespoons fresh lemon juice

2 to 3 tablespoons minced chives

Coarse salt, either kosher or sea salt, optional

Fire up the grill, bringing the heat to high (1 to 2 seconds with the hand test).

Toss the shrimp with the oil, salt, and pepper.

Warm the butter in a small skillet over low to medium heat, on the stove or at the edge of the grill. When the butter is melted, remove from the heat and stir in the lemon juice and chives. Add salt if you wish.

Grill the shrimp for 2 to 3 minutes, then turn with tongs and grill for 2 to 3 minutes more on the second side. The shrimp are done when they are opaque, with a few lightly browned edges. Serve with sauce spooned over them.

Adding a Personal Signature:

Skip the butter and serve the simply seasoned shrimp, hot or chilled, with another sauce such as:

- your favorite cocktail sauce
- mango chutney thinned with a bit of water or vinegar
- Mexican hot sauce.

SMOKY DRY-RUBBED SHRIMP

If you haven't yet discovered smoked paprika, it's time to go looking. Imported from Spain, it's a great griller's secret, especially for shrimp. If you can't find it locally, you can mail order the paprika from spanishtable.com, or try one of the other dry rubs discussed below as signature variations. Any dry rub preparation helps create a crusty surface, a perfect contrast for the shrimp's succulent interior.

Serves 4 or more

DRY RUB

1 tablespoon smoked paprika

1 teaspoon coarse salt, either kosher or sea salt

½ teaspoon chili powder

½ teaspoon onion powder

½ teaspoon brown sugar

1½ pounds medium-large to large shrimp (about 30 per pound), peeled and tails removed, and if you wish, deveined

Vegetable oil spray

Lemon or lime wedges, or capers, optional

Combine the dry rub ingredients in a large shallow bowl. Add the shrimp and rub the mixture over them well.

Fire up the grill, bringing the heat to high (1 to 2 seconds with the hand test).

Just before placing the shrimp on the grill, spray them lightly with oil. (Never spray food that is already on the grill.)

Grill shrimp for 2 to 3 minutes, then turn and grill for 2 to 3 minutes more on the second side. The shrimp are done when they are opaque, with a few lightly browned edges. Serve hot, garnished if you wish with lemon wedges.

Adding a Personal Signature:

We particularly like the smoked paprika dry rub with shrimp, but others will work fine, too:

- 1½ tablespoons sweet paprika, 1 teaspoon coarse salt, ½ teaspoon chili powder, ¼ teaspoon granulated sugar

- 2 teaspoons celery salt, 1 teaspoon freshly milled pepper, ½ teaspoon garlic powder, pinch or 2 of cayenne

- 2 teaspoons dried dill, 1 teaspoon coarse salt, 1 teaspoon grated lemon zest, ½ teaspoon freshly milled pepper.

LOUISIANA BARBECUED SHRIMP

In New Orleans barbecued shrimp isn't really barbecued. This is a grilled version of that skillet-cooked local favorite full of the fiery flavors of black pepper and Louisiana hot sauce.

Serves 4

MARINADE

½ cup Worcestershire sauce

3 tablespoons tomato-based barbecue sauce

1 tablespoon minced onion

2 garlic cloves, minced

1 tablespoon, freshly cracked pepper

1 teaspoon table salt

¼ teaspoon Tabasco sauce, or more to taste

1½ pounds medium-large to large shrimp (about 30 per pound), peeled and tails removed, and if you wish, deveined

3 tablespoons butter, preferably unsalted, in several chunks

2 tablespoons fresh lemon juice

Vegetable oil spray

Combine the marinade ingredients in a large bowl. Stir in the shrimp and let them soak in the mixture for 30 minutes at room temperature, stirring occasionally.

Fire up the grill, bringing the heat to high (1 to 2 seconds with the hand test).

Drain the marinade from the shrimp and pour it into a medium saucepan. Bring the marinade to a boil and boil vigorously for several minutes. Add the butter, stirring until it melts completely. Remove from the heat and stir in the lemon juice. Reserve as a sauce.

Arrange a sheet of nonstick grill foil, large enough to hold the shrimp in one layer, over the grill's cooking grate. If you don't have this type of foil, use a sheet of regular foil and poke holes in it every few inches with a skewer. Spray the side you'll place the shrimp on with vegetable oil spray. Place the shrimp on the foil in one layer. Grill the shrimp for 2 to 3 minutes, baste quickly with sauce, then turn and grill for 2 to 3 minutes more on the second side. The shrimp are done when they are opaque, with a few lightly browned edges.

Adding a Personal Signature:

Serve these on small, griddle-cooked corncakes or split biscuits, over a bed of long-simmered black-eyed peas, or tossed with fettucine.

SPICE-UP-YOUR-LIFE
PARTY

Louisiana Barbecued Shrimp

Grill-Roasted Oysters with Tabasco Vinaigrette (page 22)

Sliced tomatoes

Warm Potato Salad (page 163)

Piña Colada Sorbet (page 172)

GRILLED SHRIMP TACOS

Now that we're accustomed to the once-odd idea of fish tacos, it's time to jump ahead of the crowd and adopt another taco delight from the Baja California region. Since you're using Triple Sec in the marinade, you might as well pick up some tequila and make a batch of margaritas to enjoy with the shrimp.

Serves 4 or more

2 cups shredded cabbage or packaged coleslaw mix

2 tablespoons vegetable oil

1½ teaspoons table salt, or more to taste

White vinegar

1½ pounds medium-large to large shrimp (about 30 per pound), peeled and tails removed, and if you wish, deveined

Juice of 2 medium limes (3 to 4 tablespoons)

2 tablespoons Triple Sec or other orange-flavored liqueur

1½ teaspoons to 1 tablespoon Mexican hot sauce, such as Cholula

Approximately 12 corn tortillas, warmed

1 or 2 avocados, sliced in thin wedges

Additional Mexican hot sauce

Stir together in a bowl the cabbage, 1 tablespoon of the oil, at least ½ teaspoon of the salt, and a few splashes of vinegar. Let sit at room temperature.

Toss the shrimp in a large bowl with the lime juice, the remaining 1 tablespoon of oil, the Triple Sec, hot sauce to taste, and the remaining teaspoon salt. There should be just enough liquid to coat the shrimp. Let sit at room temperature, stirring occasionally.

Fire up the grill, bringing the heat to high (1 to 2 seconds with the hand test).

Drain the shrimp, discarding the marinade.

Grill the shrimp for 2 to 3 minutes, then turn and grill for 2 to 3 minutes more on the second side. The shrimp are done when they are opaque, with a few lightly browned edges. Pile the shrimp onto a platter.

Let guests assemble their own soft tacos, filling one tortilla at a time with a few shrimp, a forkful of cabbage shreds, and a couple of avocado slices. Pass the hot sauce and dig in.

BAJA DINNER

Chips and salsa

Grilled Shrimp Tacos

White rice with cilantro and grated lime zest

Black beans

Bananas with Dulce de Leche (page 150)

HOT SHRIMP SKEWERS WITH COOL GREEK SALAD

The Americanized Greek salad may elicit yawns in some food circles, but the ingredients work well together. We give the salad a makeover here, skewering tomatoes and olives with the shrimp on the grill and serving them all on romaine leaves topped with feta.

Serves 4

½ cup mayonnaise

1 to 2 tablespoons minced pepperoncini peppers (stems and seeds discarded)

24 medium-large to large shrimp (about 30 per pound), peeled and if you wish, deveined

12 cherry tomatoes

12 pitted tangy black olives, such as Kalamata

Flavorful olive oil

Coarse salt, either kosher or sea salt

1 tablespoon minced fresh dill or 1½ teaspoons dried dill

Crisp leaves from 1 large head romaine, sliced crosswise in thin ribbons

3 to 4 ounces feta cheese, crumbled (about ¾ cup)

2 pita breads, cut in 6 wedges each

Soaked bamboo skewers, preferably about 10 inches long

Stir together the mayonnaise and peppers to your taste in a small bowl. Refrigerate until serving time.

Rub the shrimp, tomatoes, and olives with a thin coat of olive oil. Sprinkle with salt and dill.

Fire up the grill, bringing the heat to high (1 to 2 seconds with the hand test).

For each diner, make 2 kebabs with 3 shrimp each. On the first, pierce the skewer down through the shrimp near its tail end. Slide a tomato onto the skewer to fit in the natural curvature of the shrimp body, and then skewer back up through the head end of the shrimp. Repeat with another shrimp, but this time skewer an olive in the hollow between the tail and the head. Repeat again with a shrimp and tomato. Make another kebab, this time using 2 olives and 1 tomato in the shrimp hollows. Repeat with the remaining skewers and ingredients.

Arrange the kebabs on the grill with the handles of the skewers off or angled away from the fire. Brush the pita wedges with oil and place near the edge of the grill to toast, taking them off as they become lightly brown and crisp. Grill the shrimp skewers for 2 to 3 minutes, then turn and grill for 2 to 3 minutes more on the second side. The kebabs are ready when the shrimp are opaque, with a few lightly browned edges.

To serve, divide the romaine among four plates, toss with enough oil to glisten, and scatter feta over them equally. Top with two skewers each (one with 2 tomatoes and one with 1 per diner). Add a spoonful of mayo to each plate along with a few pita wedges and serve immediately.

Succulent Salmon

Nothing evokes the glory of the outdoors like salmon, particularly the fresh wild Pacific salmon available in prime grilling season. Hearty but light, elemental but elegant, salmon is America's favorite fish, enjoyed by many people who shun meats and even other fish. Farm-raised salmon has helped fuel the popularity of the fish, but wild salmon has much fuller flavor and, generally, is a better choice environmentally too. Bring the wilderness home at your next party and your friends are likely to go wild over the idea.

Despite a perceived fragility, salmon thrives on the direct high, dry heat of the grill. The fire crusts the surface slightly, providing a magnificent contrast with the still translucent center. To avoid fish sticking to the grate, oil both right before you grill but not to the point where either is dripping fat into the fire. We always preheat the grate before cooking anything, but it's especially important with fish as another way of averting the same stickiness problem. If you follow these precautions and grill salmon quickly on a hot fire, you and your guests will be leaping with joy over the results.

MUSTARD-RUBBED SALMON STEAKS

Steaks are the easiest form of most fish to grill. Salmon steaks in particular contain a fair bit of flavor-filled fat, keeping them as juicy on a hot fire as a beef steak. To complement that richness here, we coat the steaks with a slightly tangy mustard seasoning paste and then add a touch of it to a butter sauce for a final fillip.

Serves 4

MUSTARD PASTE

¼ cup hot sweet mustard, or 3½ tablespoons Dijon or hot mustard and 1½ teaspoons honey

2 teaspoons minced fresh dill or 1 teaspoon dried dill

1 teaspoon cracked yellow mustard seeds

1 teaspoon coarse salt, either kosher or sea salt

Four 1-inch thick salmon steaks, about 7 to 8 ounces each

Vegetable oil spray

4 tablespoons (½ stick) butter, preferably unsalted

Coarse salt, either kosher or sea salt, optional

Dill sprigs, optional

Combine the mustard, dill, mustard seeds, and salt in a small bowl. Set aside 2 teaspoons of the mixture. Smear the rest of the paste lightly over the salmon steaks. To facilitate even cooking, toothpick the two "tails" of each salmon steak together side by side. If the "tails" are so thin that they flop over, curl them inward until they touch the main portion of the steaks and secure each with a toothpick. Let sit at room temperature.

Fire up the grill, bringing the heat to medium-high to high (2 to 3 seconds with the hand test).

Warm the butter in a small skillet at the edge of the grill and when melted, stir in the reserved mustard paste. Add salt if you wish.

Spray the steaks with the oil until well lubricated but not dripping, and transfer to the well-oiled, hot grate. Grill for about 8 minutes total, turning three times, and rotating a half-turn each time for crisscross grill marks. Don't touch or move the steaks except to rotate or turn, because getting a good sear where the fish touches the grate is essential to prevent sticking. If you get any resistance when you turn or rotate the fish, re-oil the grate. The steaks are done when just barely opaque, with a touch of darker translucence remaining at the center. Remove the toothpicks. Serve hot with a spoonful of the butter over each steak.

Adding a Personal Signature:

Replace the mustard seasoning with another paste that reflects your tastes. Some possibilities include:

- a store-bought flavored mayonnaise, such as wasabi or chipotle chile, with a little lemon juice added to the former or lime juice to the latter

- a lemon paste: puree together the zest and juice of 1 large lemon, 3 tablespoons olive oil, 3 tablespoons chopped onion, 2 garlic cloves, and 1 teaspoon coarse salt

- a ginger paste: puree together 2 ounces of fresh ginger with 1 tablespoon sugar, 1 tablespoon peanut oil, and 1 teaspoon coarse salt

THE BOSS IS COMING TO DINNER

Champagne Coolers (page 177)

Mustard-Rubbed Salmon Steaks

Orzo and Zucchini Salad (page 164)

Grilled Strawberries with Whipped Cream Cheese (page 154)

SALMON FILLETS WITH BASIL AND ORANGE

We love fresh basil with salmon, particularly in this French Caribbean–inspired preparation. Ask your fish market for center-cut fillet sections, which are the meatiest and aren't as tapered as those from other parts of the salmon. If necessary, remove thinner pieces while thicker ones remain on the grill, or whisk pieces off sooner for those who prefer it less done.

Serves 4 to 6

Four or six 5- to 6-ounce sections skin-on salmon fillet, preferably about ¾ inch thick

MARINADE
½ cup orange juice, fresh or diluted from concentrate
½ teaspoon coarse salt, either kosher or sea salt

BASIL OIL
½ cup lightly packed basil leaves
½ cup flavorful olive oil

½ teaspoon coarse salt, either kosher or sea salt

Flaky sea salt, such as Maldon, or coarse salt, either kosher or sea salt
Basil sprigs, optional

Stroke the surface of the salmon, feeling for tiny pin bones. Remove any that you find with tweezers.

Pour the orange juice into a shallow dish that will hold all the fillets in a single layer. Stir in the salt and add the fillets, skin side up.

Prepare the basil oil, pureeing the ingredients together in a food processor or blender. Set aside 2 tablespoons of the oil.

Fire up the grill, bringing the heat to high (1 to 2 seconds with the hand test).

Drain the salmon, discarding the marinade. Brush the flesh side of the fish lightly with the oil you set aside.

Transfer the fillets skin side up to the well-oiled hot grate. Grill over high heat for 2 minutes, rotating the fillets a half-turn after 1 minute for crisscross grill marks. (If the fillets are thicker than 1 inch, keep them skin side up for an additional minute, rotating after 1½ minutes.) Don't touch or move the fillets except to rotate or turn, because getting a good sear where the fish touches the grate is essential to prevent sticking. If you get any resistance when you rotate the fish, re-oil the grate. Gently turn the fillets skin side down. Brush the cooked surface lightly with enough basil oil to glisten, and continue cooking for about 4 more minutes, until the skin is very dark and crisp. The salmon is done when just barely opaque, with a touch of darker translucence remaining at the center. Arrange the fillets on plates. Drizzle the remaining oil equally over the fillets, letting some of it pool on the plates. Sprinkle with additional salt and serve, garnished with sprigs of basil if you wish.

SALMON FILLET FOR A CROWD

A full salmon fillet declares, "this is a big party." We season it simply here and serve it with two different condiments, giving everyone a chance to have it their way.

Serves 8 to 10

2½ to 2¾-pound whole skin-on salmon fillet, preferably about ¾-inch thick and no more than about 16 inches long

Coarse salt, either kosher or sea salt

Coarsely ground pepper

Olive oil or vegetable oil

LEMON-HORSERADISH CRÈME FRAÎCHE

1 cup crème fraîche, preferably, or sour cream

1 tablespoon prepared horseradish, or more to taste

Juice and finely shredded zest of 1 small lemon (save a few shreds of zest to top the salmon at the end)

Pinch or 2 coarse salt, either kosher or sea salt

CUCUMBER-SCALLION RELISH

1 large cucumber, preferably an English or European variety, peeled, seeded, and finely diced

4 scallions, roots and limp tops trimmed, minced

2 tablespoons olive oil or vegetable oil

1½ teaspoons white vinegar

¼ teaspoon coarse salt, either kosher or sea salt, or more to taste

Stroke the surface of the salmon, feeling for tiny pin bones. Remove any that you find with tweezers. To facilitate even cooking, make diagonal slashes down through the salmon, 2 to 3 inches apart, from one side to the other, without cutting through the skin. (If you know how many guests you'll be serving, you can adjust the slashes in width somewhat to delineate each person's portion.) Generously salt and pepper the salmon, rubbing the seasonings into the diagonal cuts too. Brush with a light coat of oil. Cover the salmon and let it sit at room temperature for about 30 minutes.

Prepare the two condiments. Stir together the lemon-horseradish crème fraîche ingredients in one bowl, and the cucumber-scallion relish in another. Refrigerate until serving time.

process. If you see a billowing dark cloud emerging, or any other sign that the board is burning instead of smoldering, open the grill *carefully* and douse any flames with a spray bottle of water. If using a gas grill, aim at the wood rather than at the burners.

After the salmon has cooked for 8 to 10 minutes, turn off or shut down the heat and let the salmon sit in the covered grill for 8 to 10 minutes longer. (The plank shields the salmon from the heat, making the cooking time longer than if you were cooking it directly.) The smoke will brown the surface, and the high heat will nicely crisp it, an effect enhanced by the coarse seasonings. The salmon is done when just barely opaque, with a touch of darker translucence remaining at the center.

Use a pair of heatproof mitts, preferably easily rinsable, to remove the plank with the salmon from the grill. Transfer the plank to an upside down baking sheet placed on a work surface near the grill. The bottom of the plank will be sooty, so be careful about what you put it on, even after it's cooled.

Definitely show off your salmon on the plank before divvying it up. The easiest way to serve is to bring the plates to the plank. If you want to serve the salmon at the table, cover the baking sheet with a washable large cloth napkin or other fabric that can be cleaned easily. Then place the plank with the salmon on the napkin and take the whole thing to the table to serve.

Be sure to let the plank cool completely before you stash it somewhere or toss it out. Rinse well, whether you plan to use it again or not.

PAELLA and Jambalaya

When you want to do something out of the ordinary, make paella or jambalaya. They taste fantastic with grilled ingredients, look great with their mélange of colors and textures, and show that you put forward your best effort. They require more time and organization than cooking a few chicken breasts, but you won't find a better return anywhere for the investment of energy.

Paella originated in Spain as an outdoor dish, cooked in an open pan over a wood fire, and in Louisiana bayou country, jambalaya seems meant for the same setting. Traditional versions of these rice-based dishes don't feature grilled ingredients, but they work wonderfully in both cases. You can even cook the rice itself on the grill, if you wish, using the grate as a stovetop burner. Whether you do it all outdoors or just parts of it, paella and jambalaya will seem very much at home on your patio. Sprinkle in some friends and let the good times roll.

SEAFOOD PAELLA WITH *AILLOLI*

You can prepare paella in a large skillet, but if you like it as much as we do, get an actual paella pan from a local kitchen store or perhaps spanishtable.com. A fourteen-inch pan is ideal for this and the following recipe. Also for premier flavor, use the best available stock in both paella and jambalaya, preferably homemade or at least a good store-bought version.

Serves 8 to 10

AILLOLI

4 to 6 plump garlic cloves, chopped coarsely by hand

1½ teaspoons coarse salt, either kosher or sea salt

2 egg yolks, at room temperature

2 tablespoons fresh lemon juice

1 cup mild-flavored olive oil

¼ cup vegetable oil

FOR THE GRILL

1 pound medium (about 36 per pound) shrimp, peeled and, if you wish, deveined

½ pound cleaned small squid bodies, preferably about 3 inches long, with tentacles separated, or ½ pound squid steaks

Flavorful olive oil

Coarse salt, either kosher or sea salt

Freshly milled pepper

16 hard-shell clams such as cherrystones or littlenecks, or mussels, cleaned

FOR THE PAN

5 cups chicken stock

1 cup seafood stock or bottled clam juice

1½ teaspoons crumbled saffron threads

¼ cup olive oil

¼ pound pancetta, chopped

1 medium red onion, diced

1 medium red bell pepper, diced

1 medium green bell pepper, diced

2 tablespoons minced garlic

3 cups short-grain rice, such as Bomba or Arborio

Coarse salt, either kosher or sea salt

¾ cup pitted briny green olives, or black olives, or a combination

½ cup baby peas, fresh or frozen (unthawed)

⅓ cup minced fresh parsley, preferably flat leaf

Prepare the ailloli. Using a wooden spoon, crush the garlic together with the salt in a medium bowl. Add the egg yolks and, switching utensils, whisk until they lighten to a pale yellow. Continue whisking and pour in the lemon juice. When the mixture is frothy, gradually add the oils in a steady stream until a mayonnaise consistency is reached. Adjust the salt and refrigerate until serving time.

Rub the shrimp and squid lightly with oil and season with salt and pepper. Cover them and let sit at room temperature, along with the clams, while you start the rice.

Fire up the grill, bringing the heat to high (1 to 2 seconds with the hand test). If you would like to cook the rice over the grill fire, instead of on a sideburner or stovetop, you'll need the capability for medium-low heat as well.

Begin the rice. Stir together the stocks and the saffron and let the mixture stand. Warm the oil in a 12- to 14-inch paella pan or skillet over medium heat. Stir in the pancetta, onion, bell peppers, and garlic, and sauté several minutes until the pancetta is beginning to crisp and the vegetables are just tender. Stir in the rice and continue cooking until translucent, about 4 to 5 minutes. Give the stock a stir and pour it over the rice. Add salt to taste. Cook the rice over medium-low heat uncovered, without stirring, until the liquid is absorbed, about 20 minutes. After about 15 minutes of cooking, insert a spoon or spatula straight down into the rice in several places, to make sure that the rice isn't browning on the bottom in one spot before the liquid is absorbed in others. Shift the position of the pan over the heat if it is getting more done in one spot than others. When done, the liquid should be absorbed and the rice should be tender but have the barest hint of crust on the bottom and sides.

While the rice cooks, grill the seafood. Arrange the clams on the grill and cook on high heat until they pop open wide, about 8 to 10 minutes. Discard any that refuse to open within a couple of minutes of the others. Remove them from the grill carefully to avoid losing the juices in the shells. Place them on the hot rice. Grill the shrimp and squid over high heat for a total of about 4 minutes, turning to cook on all sides. The squid tentacles will likely be ready first, so take them off as soon as they firm. When done, the shrimp should be pink and opaque with lightly charred edges and the squid bodies firm but tender. Heap

the shrimp over the rice. Slice the squid bodies into thin rings and add them to the rice.

Stir the grilled ingredients into the rice and scatter with the olives, peas, and parsley. Serve immediately or cover with foil and keep warm in a low oven or on a corner of the grill. If using a paella pan, serve from the pan. If using a skillet, spoon out onto a platter and then serve. In either case, pass the ailloli on the side.

Adding a Personal Signature:

You can make all kinds of modifications in a dish like this. Add more of a favorite seafood, perhaps the shrimp, and less of one that you can't find or don't like as much. Replace one of the seafood choices with another, such as plump scallops cooked in the same fashion as the shrimp. Leave out the pancetta and add more olive oil if you're adverse to meat, or if you're the opposite, add some slices of pre-cooked Spanish chorizo or grilled Italian sausage. Use black rice instead of white for the base, which really makes the seafood stand out. The darker rice may require a few extra minutes of cooking, so add a bit more chicken stock to the paella if the rice begins to get dry before it is tender.

BARCELONA BARBECUE

Grilled Pears with Serrano Ham and Cabrales Blue Crumbles (page 17)

Seafood Paella with Ailloli

Pan de Tomate (page 167)

Crema catalana or flan

Sangria Blanca (page 176)

CHICKEN-CHORIZO PAELLA

This paella's a bit richer and heartier than the seafood version, though not heavy or inappropriate for a summer meal.

Serves 8 to 12

FOR THE GRILL

1¼ pounds boneless, skinless chicken breasts, pounded ½ inch thick

Flavorful olive oil

Coarse salt, either kosher or sea salt

Freshly milled pepper

1 pound (about 6 links) uncooked Spanish chorizo or other uncooked spicy sausage links, such as Italian sausage or Mexican chorizo

FOR THE PAN

6 cups chicken stock

1½ teaspoons crumbled saffron threads

¼ cup plus 1 tablespoon flavorful olive oil

1 medium red onion, diced

1 medium red bell pepper, diced

1 medium green bell pepper, diced

2 tablespoons minced garlic

One or two 3- to 4-inch rosemary sprigs

3 cups short-grain rice, such as Bomba or Arborio

¾ cup pitted briny green olives, or black olives, or a combination

1 cup slivered cooked artichoke hearts or bottoms

¼ cup minced fresh parsley, preferably flat leaf

Additional rosemary sprigs, optional

Rub the chicken breasts lightly with oil, then sprinkle with salt and pepper. Cover and let the chicken and chorizo sit at room temperature while you prepare the rice.

Fire up the grill, bringing the heat to medium (4 to 5 seconds with the hand test). If you would like to cook the rice over the grill fire, instead of on a sideburner or stovetop, you'll need the capability for medium-low heat as well.

Begin the rice. Stir together the stock and the saffron and let the mixture stand. Warm the oil in a 12- to 14-inch paella pan or skillet over medium heat. Stir in the onion, bell peppers, garlic, and rosemary and sauté several minutes until softened. Stir in the rice and continue cooking until just translucent, about 4 to 5 minutes. Give the stock a stir and pour over the rice. Add salt to taste. Cook the rice over medium-low heat uncovered, without stirring, until the liquid is absorbed, about 20 minutes. After about 15 minutes of cooking, insert a spoon or spatula straight down into the rice in several places, to make sure that the rice isn't browning on the bottom in one spot before the liquid is absorbed in others. Shift the position of the pan over the heat if it is getting more done in one spot than others. When done, the liquid should be absorbed and the rice should be tender but have the barest hint of crust on the bottom and sides.

While the rice cooks, grill the chicken and chorizo over medium heat. Grill the chicken for 10 to 12 minutes total. Turn onto each side twice, rotating the breasts a half-turn each time for crisscross grill marks. The chicken is ready when it is white throughout but still juicy. The chorizo is ready when lightly crusted and cooked through, about 8 to 10 minutes depending on the size of the links. Slice the chicken into bite-size pieces and the chorizo into thin half-moons and scatter over the rice.

Stir the chicken and chorizo into the rice, remove the cooked rosemary, and scatter the olives, artichokes, and parsley over it. Serve immediately, or cover with foil and keep warm in a low oven or on a corner of the grill. Garnish if you like with fresh rosemary sprigs. If using a paella pan, serve from the pan. If using a skillet, spoon out onto a platter and then serve.

Adding a Personal Signature:

As with the previous paella, mix and match as you wish. Use peas here instead of artichokes, add another favorite sausage, substitute duck breasts (grilled as in the following jambalaya recipe) or rabbit loin for the chicken, replace the rosemary with tarragon. Bear in mind that you want to end up with an appealing mix of colors and textures.

DUCK JAMBALAYA

Jambalaya is traditionally cooked covered, often in an old iron pot hanging over a fire, but it translates well to a grill party with a few modifications. If you don't care for duck, or find it gaspingly expensive in local stores, substitute boneless, skinless chicken breasts, ignoring the instructions below regarding the duck skin.

Serves 8 as a main dish

FOR THE GRILL

4 individual duck breasts, 6 to 7 ounces each

Coarse salt, either kosher or sea salt

Freshly milled pepper

7 to 8 ounces andouille sausage links or other smoked pork sausage links, such as kielbasa

FOR THE POT

3 tablespoons vegetable oil

1½ cups chopped onions

¼ pound tasso (Cajun seasoning ham), country ham, or other smoky ham, minced

1½ cups minced celery

1 large green bell pepper, chopped

½ red bell pepper, chopped

2 plump garlic cloves, minced

2 cups uncooked long-grain rice

3 cups chicken stock

¼ teaspoon Tabasco sauce or other Louisiana hot sauce, or more to taste

1 dried bay leaf

1 teaspoon dry mustard powder

1½ teaspoons table salt

¾ teaspoon crumbled dried thyme

½ teaspoon freshly milled pepper

A handful of thin-sliced scallion rings, green and white portions both

If the duck breast skin is any thicker than ¼ inch, trim it to that thickness with a sharp knife, shearing off portions as needed. Also slice off any portions of skin or fat that hang beyond the top edge of the meat. Make crisscross cuts down through the remaining skin on the breasts. Make the cuts about ½ inch apart, through the skin but not into the flesh. This will help the seasonings flavor the duck more fully, and during cooking, it promotes gradual and easy rendering of fat. Rub the salt and pepper over the breasts, cover them, and let them and the andouille sit at room temperature.

Fire up the grill, bringing the heat to medium (4 to 5 seconds with the hand test). You will need enough grate space to be able to move the duck breasts around as needed when the inevitable and theatrical flare-ups occur. If you would like to cook the rice over the grill fire, instead of on a sideburner or stovetop, you'll need the capability for medium-low heat as well.

Begin the rice. Warm the oil in a heavy 8- to 10-inch skillet over high heat. Mix in the onions and tasso, and sauté until the onion is well-browned but not burned, 8 to 10 minutes. Add the celery, bell peppers, and garlic, reduce the heat to medium, and continue cooking until the vegetables are softened, about 5 additional minutes. Stir in the rice and cook for about 3 minutes longer, until the grains are translucent. Pour in the stock and add the remaining seasonings. Bring just to a boil, then reduce the heat to medium-low. Cover and cook until the rice is tender and the liquid is absorbed, 18 to 20 minutes, stirring up from the bottom once about half-way through the cooking.

While the rice cooks, grill the duck breasts and andouille over medium heat. Transfer the breasts to the grill skin side down. Grill over medium heat for 4 to 6 minutes, watching carefully and moving around as needed to avoid flare-ups. Cook until the skin is deep golden brown and crisp. Turn the breasts and grill skin side up for an additional 3 to 4 minutes for medium, then slice thinly so that each piece has some of the crisp skin. Grill the andouille until nicely brown and a bit crisp, about 6 to 10 minutes, depending on size. Slice the andouille into thin half-moons.

Remove the rice from the heat when done, and let it sit covered for 10 minutes. Stir the andouille and any juice from it and the duck into the rice. Remove the bay leaf from the rice. Spoon jambalaya into a large bowl or onto plates. Arrange duck slices on top, dot with scallions, and serve.

MARDI GRAS PARTY

Grill-Roasted Oysters with Tabasco Vinaigrette (page 22)

Steamed artichokes with lemon butter

Duck Jambalaya

Bread pudding with bourbon sauce

Sazeracs

VEGETABLE JAMBALAYA

A lively and hearty main dish, this can also serve as a special side dish. We grill the vegetables first, to deepen their flavor, and then finish cooking them with the rice mixture.

Serves 8 as a main dish

FOR THE GRILL

Two 6- to 6½-ounce jars or one 12-ounce jar marinated artichoke hearts, drained, oil reserved

¼ teaspoon Tabasco sauce or other Louisiana hot sauce

1 large red bell pepper

1 large green bell pepper

2 large onions, sliced ⅓-inch thick

4 red-ripe plum tomatoes, halved lengthwise

Coarse salt, either kosher or sea salt

1½ cups minced celery

2 plump garlic cloves, minced

2 cups uncooked long-grain rice

3 cups chicken stock

2 dried bay leaves

1½ teaspoons table salt

¾ teaspoon dry mustard powder

¾ teaspoon crumbled dried thyme

Additional Tabasco sauce or other Louisiana hot sauce

FOR THE POT

3 tablespoons vegetable oil

¼ pound tasso (Cajun seasoning ham), country ham, other smoky ham, or a smoky chicken sausage, minced

Fire up the grill, bringing the heat to medium (4 to 5 seconds with the hand test). If you would like to cook the rice over the grill fire, instead of on a sideburner or stovetop, you'll need the capability for medium-low heat as well.

Mix the oil drained from the artichoke hearts with the hot sauce and brush it over the whole bell peppers, the onions, and tomatoes. Grill the vegetables, in batches if necessary. Arrange the tomatoes cut side down to start. Cook until tender, removing each vegetable as it is done.

Plan on grilling times of 12 to 15 minutes for the peppers and the onion slices and 4 to 6 minutes for the tomatoes and artichoke hearts. Turn the peppers on all sides to cook evenly, and the rest of the vegetables three times.

Transfer the peppers to a plastic bag and close to let them steam and loosen the skin. When cool enough to handle, pull off any loose charred pieces of skin. Dice the peppers, discarding the seeds and stem. Dice the onion slices and the tomatoes, keeping them separate.

Warm the oil in a large heavy skillet over high heat. Mix in the grilled onion and the tasso, and sauté until the onion is golden and very tender, about 5 minutes. Add the grilled peppers and tomatoes with their juices, and the celery and garlic. Reduce the heat to medium, and continue cooking until the celery is tender and most of the liquid from the other vegetables has evaporated, about 5 additional minutes. Stir in the rice and cook for about 3 minutes longer, until the grains are translucent. Pour in the stock and add the remaining seasonings. Bring just to a boil, then reduce the heat to medium-low. Cover and cook until the rice is tender and the liquid is absorbed, 18 to 20 minutes, stirring up from the bottom once about half-way through the cooking. Remove the jambalaya from the heat, stir in the artichoke hearts, and let it sit covered for 10 minutes. Remove the bay leaf. Spoon the jambalaya into a large bowl or onto plates and serve.

Adding a Personal Signature:

Serve the jambalaya over or under grilled chicken breasts, sausages, or pork chops, or alongside Classic Crusty Pork Tenderloin (page 74) or Grill-Roasted Oysters with Tabasco Vinaigrette (page 22). Use it as a stuffing for baked plump red bell peppers or beefsteak tomatoes, or steamed hollowed-out zucchini or chayote boats.

Fired-Up Fruit for Dessert

Fruit always makes a good dessert, whether you serve it simply sliced with cheese or baked into a pie. At a casual summer cookout, we like to grill the fruit. Grilling it wraps up the meal with an unusual flourish and adds depth to the fruit flavor, caramelizing sugar on the surface, softening the texture, and releasing the sweet juices.

Do any necessary prep work in advance so you're ready to grill when the time comes. With a gas grill, simply shut down after you've cooked the main course and then fire up again later. If you're cooking on charcoal, try to time your dinner to keep the fire hot enough for a second round of grilling. Close the cover when the entrée is done, shut down the vents almost fully, and then as soon as you finish the main course, open everything again and put on the fruit. If the cooking temperature has fallen below medium—the desired level—just grill the fruit a little longer than the recipe says. With either gas or charcoal, the grilling is a snap but looks absolutely brilliant to guests.

BANANAS WITH DULCE DE LECHE

You can find bananas anywhere, any time of year, and always at reasonable prices, making them perfect for the grill repertoire. Warming bananas makes them meltingly luscious, so appealing that people who don't like them raw may end up eating a bowlful. Put a few extras on the grill; they'll likely disappear.

Serves 4

4 tablespoons butter, preferably unsalted	4 medium bananas
1 tablespoon sugar	¾ cup store-bought dulce de leche or other caramel sauce
½ teaspoon pure vanilla extract	

GRILLED DESSERT BUFFET

Bananas with Dulce de Leche

Passionate Mangos (page 152)

Grilled Strawberries with Whipped Cream Cheese (page 154)

Piña Colada Sorbet (page 172)

Ginger Blondies (page 169) or bakery brownies

Warm the butter and sugar together in a small skillet over medium heat, until the butter is melted and the sugar dissolved. Stir in the vanilla and remove from the heat, but keep warm.

Fire up the grill, bringing the heat to medium (4 to 5 seconds with the hand test).

Just before grilling, halve the bananas lengthwise, still in their skins. Brush the cut sides of the bananas with about one-half of the melted butter. Warm the dulce de leche sauce in a small pan over low heat, either at the edge of the grill or over the stove.

Transfer the bananas to the grill cut side down. Grill the bananas for 3 to 4 minutes. Turn the bananas skin side down and brush the cut surfaces with the remaining butter. Grill for 2 to 3 additional minutes, until soft and lightly golden. The skins will be sagging by this time. Remove and discard the skins from the bananas and cut into chunks. Arrange in bowls, spoon the sauce over equally, and serve.

Adding a Personal Signature:

This is one to play with. Add a chocolate or white chocolate sauce. Mix a little light or dark rum into the dulce de leche. Sprinkle the dish with pecans, walnuts, or almonds, plain or candied. Scatter with chopped toffee or shavings of dark chocolate. Crown with whipped cream, or arrange over pound cake.

GRILLED APPLES WITH ROQUEFORT BUTTER

Desserts with savory elements are gaining increasing favor. Cheese with fruit is the classic combo and often still the best. These apple wedges would also make a worthy side dish for grilled pork tenderloin or Spanish Leg of Lamb (page 92).

Serves 4 to 6

ROQUEFORT BUTTER

6 tablespoons unsalted butter

2 teaspoons brown sugar

2 to 3 tablespoons crumbled Roquefort or other blue cheese

4 medium apples, such as Fuji or Rome Beauty, which hold their shape when cooked

Metal skewers, optional

Orange slices, strawberries, or mint sprigs, optional

Prepare the Roquefort butter, melting the butter and brown sugar together in a small skillet over medium heat. Stir in the cheese and remove from the heat when melted.

Peel and core the apples, cutting each into 1-inch thick wedges. Thread the apples onto skewers, if you wish, or plan to lay them on a small-mesh grill rack or grill foil. Brush on all sides with just enough of the Roquefort butter to coat, and set aside until you're ready for dessert.

Fire up the grill, bringing the heat to medium (4 to 5 seconds with the hand test).

Grill the apples for 10 to 12 minutes, turning on all sides, until tender and lightly brown. Keep the butter warm over the edge of the grill. In the last couple of minutes of cooking, baste the apples again with the butter. Remove the apples from the skewers if needed. Divide the apples among serving plates and drizzle with any remaining butter. Serve immediately. Add a touch of color to the plates with orange slices or another garnish, if you wish.

PASSIONATE MANGOS

We wouldn't turn down a mango after a meal anytime, but they make an especially nice finish to a Mexican, Caribbean, or Asian-accented dinner. If you have nut oil on hand, it's a nice subtle flavor addition, but don't feel you need to go hunting for it otherwise. Fresh passion fruit adds an exotic floral note to the mango, but the more common canned nectar will also work. If you can't find either, just substitute a few squeezes of lime juice.

Serves 4 or more	4 large mangos Nut oil, such as almond or macadamia nut, or vegetable oil	1 passion fruit, halved, or a 6-ounce can passion fruit nectar

Halve the mangos: Stand one up vertically and slice down from the top center until you feel the wide, flat seed. Cut down around the curve of the seed, keeping the knife as close to it as possible. Cut down the other side of the seed in the same way. Repeat with the other mangos. Rub the cut surface lightly with oil.

Fire up the grill, bringing the heat to medium (4 to 5 seconds with the hand test.)

Transfer the mango halves to the grill skin side up. Cook for 5 to 7 minutes, until soft with a few brown edges. When cool enough to handle, make parallel cuts ½ inch apart down through the cut side to but not through the skin. Make a second set of cuts perpendicular to the first cuts, forming a crosshatch pattern. Push up under the mango half from the skin side, so that the mango flesh will pop up and spread open like a porcupine's quills. Repeat with the rest of the mangos. Arrange two mango halves on each plate. Squeeze the passion fruit equally over the mango halves and serve.

Adding a Personal Signature:

Peel and cube the mangos instead and skewer them, maybe with a few other soft-textured fruits such as pineapple or corpulent pitted cherries. Coat with the oil, grill until soft, and then top with the juice as before.

HONEYED FIGS

These taste wonderful with any type of honey, from a mild version like orange blossom to a deeply flavored lavender honey.

Serves 4 or more	⅓ cup honey	12 plump fresh figs, halved vertically
	1 tablespoon hot water	Vegetable oil spray

Stir together the honey and hot water in a small bowl.

Dip the cut side of each fig into the honey.

Fire up the grill, bringing the heat to medium (4 to 5 seconds with the hand test).

Spray the figs with the oil and transfer to the grill cut side down. Grill for 5 to 7 minutes, turning once and brushing if you wish with any remaining honey. The figs are ready when soft and oozing juice.

GRILLED STRAWBERRIES WITH WHIPPED CREAM CHEESE

Today's supermarket strawberries, grown for shipping, look beautiful but are usually too sturdy to exude much juice or flavor. Grilling softens the fruit and releases its juices. Add a little sugar and some creamy light cheese for dunking, and the berries get as close to perfect as they can be. For a more lavish dessert, serve them with slices of pound cake or angel food cake, brushed with butter and toasted over the fire.

Serves 6

8 ounces mascarpone cheese, softened

1½ pounds (about 3 pints) medium to large strawberries

Bamboo skewers, 2 for each kebab, soaked

2 tablespoons butter

½ cup vanilla syrup (the type used in coffee and other beverages)

1 to 2 tablespoons water, optional

SPRING SUPPER

Pea soup with mint

All-American Barbecued Chicken Breasts (page 100)

Couscous

Grilled Strawberries with Whipped Cream Cheese

Whisk the cheese briefly until it is easily spoonable.

Thread the strawberries on side-by-side skewers, about 4 to 6 berries per serving. Arrange on a platter or baking sheet. Warm the butter and syrup together in a small skillet on the edge of the grill and stir until the butter is melted. If the mixture is too thick to brush easily, add water as needed. Brush berries well with the mixture.

Fire up the grill, bringing the heat to medium (4 to 5 seconds with the hand test).

Transfer the kebabs to the grill. Cook the berries for 6 to 8 minutes, turning occasionally to grill on all sides until tender and oozing juice. Remove the skewers from the grill, drizzle with the remaining syrup, and serve, on or off the skewers, with a rounded tablespoon of cheese on the side.

Salads, Sides, Sweets, and Drinks

When you're grilling for friends, the most important food at the party is what you grill. If you're really rushed, you can take shortcuts with the rest of the meal, perhaps serving potato salad and dill pickles from a good deli along with a favorite store-bought ice cream for dessert.

While the easy out is an option, don't take that route without a good reason. Homemade dishes always seem more special and they usually taste that way, too. All the ones in this chapter combine simplicity of preparation with authentic, homey flavors. They take little extra effort once you're committed to hosting friends, but we've decked them out sufficiently to make your guests think you worked a little culinary magic just for them.

BLT SALAD WITH WARM BACON DRESSING

Many of us now grill year-round, but the height of the outdoor cooking season still coincides with the arrival of summer's farm-fresh tomatoes. Buy local tomatoes for this salad if at all possible—at farmers' markets, road-side stands, or produce departments that support area agriculture—and don't store them in the refrigerator, which contributes to the tennis ball texture that afflicts so many supermarket versions.

Serves 6

DRESSING

3 slices uncooked bacon, chopped

1 small shallot, minced

3 tablespoons mild-flavored olive oil

1 to 2 tablespoons white vinegar

¼ teaspoon sugar

2½ pounds vine-ripened tomatoes, preferably of different varieties, colors, and sizes

Flaky sea salt, such as Maldon, or coarse salt, either kosher or sea salt

Coarsely ground pepper

2 handfuls mixed baby greens

Prepare the dressing, frying the bacon in a skillet over medium heat until crisp. Remove the bacon with a slotted spoon and drain it on paper towels. Add the shallot to the drippings and sauté for a minute or two until just soft. Whisk in the remaining ingredients and reserve.

Slice each tomato into 3 or 4 corpulent rounds, avoiding any tough yellowish core from the top center of the tomatoes. As neatly as possible with soupy, ripe tomatoes, transfer them to individual salad plates and stack them, from larger sizes to smaller, and with some of each color in each stack. As you build, moisten the surface of each with a bit of dressing, several bacon crumbles, and a few grains of salt and pepper. You're not after something that appears to come out of a fancy restaurant kitchen, but something a little more rough-and-tumble. Tuck greens in around the bottom. Spoon the remaining dressing over the tops of the salads equally, scatter on any remaining bacon, a little more salt and pepper, and serve at room temperature.

APPLE SLAW WITH TARRAGON DRESSING

As long as they are kept chilled, cabbage salads hold up well for making ahead and serving later. The herb and apple additions here perk up this old warhorse without changing its long-loved essence.

Serves 8 or more

DRESSING

1 cup mayonnaise

½ cup sour cream

6 tablespoons tarragon-flavored white wine vinegar

3 tablespoons sugar

1½ teaspoons table salt

1 teaspoon freshly milled pepper

1 small head green cabbage, shredded

¼ head red cabbage, shredded

3 tablespoons minced fresh tarragon

2 crisp, tangy medium apples, such as Granny Smith

SIMPLE SUNDAY SUPPER

Chicken with Sage Sandwich (page 108)

Apple Slaw with Tarragon Dressing

Ginger Blondies (page 169)

Prepare the dressing, whisking together the ingredients in a medium bowl.

Prepare the slaw, stirring together the two cabbages and tarragon in a large bowl. Toss with the dressing. Grate the apples, stirring each one into the dressed cabbage immediately after grating, to avoid turning brown. (If your grater is the one you got for a wedding present in 1983, it may be time for a replacement. A dull grater makes more work of shredding the apple skins.)

Cover and refrigerate, serving within a couple of hours for best flavor.

EASY BAKED BEANS

Few grill parties seem complete without beans. Sometimes we opt for white beans or chickpeas simmered for hours and served in a vinaigrette, but for more impromptu get-togethers, this spiffed-up version of canned baked beans offers a lot of flavor. They're a bit more Tucson than Boston in seasoning.

Serves 6 to 8

3 or 4 slices uncooked bacon, diced

1 medium onion, chopped fine

Three 16-ounce cans baked beans, or one 28-ounce and one 16-ounce can

¾ cup chili sauce (the ketchup-style sauce), tomato-based barbecue sauce, or chipotle ketchup

2 tablespoons brown sugar, or more to taste

1½ tablespoons Worcestershire sauce

1½ tablespoons prepared yellow or Dijon mustard

½ teaspoon crushed dried red chile flakes

½ teaspoon ground cumin

Preheat the oven to 350°F.

Sauté the bacon in an ovenproof skillet over medium heat for 5 minutes, until limp and just beginning to brown. Stir in the onion and continue cooking the mixture until the onions are translucent, about 5 additional minutes. Add the rest of the ingredients. Taste and adjust the seasoning, adding more brown sugar if you prefer sweeter beans. Bake uncovered 45 to 50 minutes, until bubbly throughout with a bit of browned crust at the edges. Serve hot. The beans reheat superbly.

Adding a Personal Signature:

If you've got beer to spare, pour anywhere from a cup to a can into the beans, or if you're short on beer but like the idea, stir in some dark rum to taste. Molasses or maple syrup or dark corn syrup can be combined with the brown sugar or even substituted for it. For meatier beans, add several big handfuls of a chopped grilled sausage, or better yet, shredded smoked beef brisket or pork rib meat. On the other hand, you can leave out meat entirely, replacing the bacon with a couple of tablespoons of vegetable oil or butter for sautéing the onion.

MOROCCAN CARROT SALAD

Carrot salads always remind us pleasantly of childhood cookouts, but this version adds a Moroccan note that we never would have contemplated in our youth in mid-century suburban America.

Serves 6

SALAD

6 large carrots (1 to 1¼ pounds), shredded

¾ cup white raisins

½ medium green bell pepper, diced fine

DRESSING

6 tablespoons orange-flavored olive oil (such as O brand), other olive oil, or roasted peanut oil

2 tablespoons cider vinegar

2 teaspoons sugar

¾ teaspoon table salt

½ teaspoon curry powder, or more to taste

¼ teaspoon ground cumin

Mix together the salad ingredients in a large bowl.

Prepare the dressing, whisking the ingredients together in a small bowl. Pour the dressing over the salad and toss it well. Refrigerate the salad at least 30 minutes and up to overnight. Serve chilled.

WARM POTATO SALAD

With a hint of smoke and spice, this potato salad fits beautifully into any outdoor dinner. Hearty enough for burgers, it also dresses up for a more elegant meal because of its French-style, mayo-less dressing.

Serves 6 to 8

3 tablespoons white wine vinegar

2 to 3 tablespoons minced shallots

2½ pounds small waxy potatoes, such as fingerlings or Yukon gold

1½ to 2 tablespoons dry shrimp-boil or crab-boil seasoning, such as Zatarain's or Old Bay

3 or 4 slices crisp-cooked bacon, crumbled

1 large celery stalk, minced

¼ cup mild-flavored olive oil or vegetable oil, or more to taste

Coarse salt and freshly milled pepper, optional

Combine the vinegar and shallots in a broad serving bowl. Let the mixture sit while you cook the potatoes.

Unless the potatoes are truly bite-size, halve them or otherwise cut them into manageable chunks. Put the potatoes and the shrimp boil in a large pot of warm, lightly salted water. Bring to a boil, then reduce the heat to medium and simmer until the potatoes are easily pierced with a fork, 15 to 20 minutes. Drain off the water, then return the pot of potatoes to lowest heat for a couple of minutes, shaking the pot to help evaporate water from the potatoes. Remove from the heat, place a clean dish towel over the pot, and cover it with the lid for a couple of minutes to further eliminate moisture.

Fold the still-warm potatoes into the vinegar mixture with a light hand. Add the bacon and celery. Drizzle in the oil until the mixture is lightly coated. If the potatoes taste too strongly of vinegar, add another tablespoon or two of oil, and salt and pepper if needed. Combine lightly again and serve warm or at room temperature.

ORZO AND ZUCCHINI SALAD

Orzo's a great little party pasta. It holds its shape better than rice, which it resembles, if you get busy and over-cook it, and it clumps less than couscous, another of our other favorite salad starches. Here the pasta mixes with bright bits of zucchini in a sunny dressing.

Serves 6

2 medium zucchini (1 to 1¼ pounds total), unpeeled

1 teaspoon coarse salt, either kosher or sea salt

8 ounces (1 cup) orzo pasta

¼ cup olive oil

½ cup lightly packed slivered fresh mint leaves

1 tablespoon fresh lemon juice, or more to taste

Pinch of cumin

Coarse salt, either kosher or sea salt

Freshly milled pepper

¼ cup pine nuts, toasted, optional

Shred the zucchini on the large holes of a box grater. Mix in a bowl with the salt and set aside for 15 to 20 minutes to release much of the vegetable's moisture.

While the zucchini sits, cook the orzo according to the package directions. Do not overcook. Drain the pasta well and dump it into a mixing bowl. Stir in the oil and let the mixture cool several minutes.

Place the zucchini on a clean dish towel and ring it out over the sink until no more watery liquid comes out. Stir the zucchini and mint into the orzo, then season with lemon juice, cumin, salt, and pepper. Refrigerate the salad for at least 30 minutes. If using the pine nuts, stir them in shortly before serving. Serve chilled.

Adding a Personal Signature:

Good additions include bits of fresh mozzarella, cucumber cubes, and little tomatoes. Substitute basil for the mint or slivered almonds for the pine nuts. Make the salad a bed for Rosemary and Mint Lamb Burgers (page 65) instead of using the bread.

GREAT GREEN SALADS

Once you've perfected your grill favorites, you won't want to serve them with packaged salad greens and bottled dressing. Here are some fresh combinations to get you thinking about the possibilities. Just buy a few fine quality oils, and a couple of interesting vinegars, and start playing.

Serves as many as you like

Frisée or arugula tossed with lemon juice and olive oil

Butter lettuce with avocado, pepitas (hulled pumpkin seeds) or pine nuts, maybe with some cress or mint, and lime vinaigrette

Endive and frisée with hazelnuts and finely minced celery topped with hazelnut oil vinaigrette

Arugula or watercress with chopped dates, crisp bacon crumbles, big shreds of Parmesan, and sherry vinaigrette

Shredded romaine with shredded carrots and zucchini and green peppercorn vinaigrette

Butter lettuce or watercress with tangerine sections and slivered almonds, doused lightly with tangerine vinaigrette

Spinach and fresh basil leaves with cooked bacon or pancetta bits and shallot vinaigrette

Crisp romaine hearts with Maytag blue cheese dressing and a sprinkling of toasted walnuts

An ice-cold wedge of iceberg with Thousand Island dressing perked up with chili powder or a little salsa

AND ALWAYS:

Flaky sea salt, such as Maldon, or coarse salt, either kosher or sea salt

Freshly milled pepper

Serve immediately after assembling.

CORN PUDDING

Most of our suggested sides are served cold or at room temperature, so that you can make them ahead and pull them out at the appropriate time. For a hot exception to the rule, we opt for corn pudding. When plump fresh-picked ears of sweet corn signal the arrival of high summer, we always whip up a few batches of this. It's also good at other times of the year, made with frozen corn, although you lose the delicious milky scrapings that come from the fresh ears.

Serves 6

Butter or vegetable oil spray

2 large eggs

1 cup half-and-half

¾ teaspoon table salt, or more to taste

⅛ teaspoon ground white pepper

Pinch of grated or ground nutmeg

8 to 10 ears fresh sweet corn, kernels and milky scrapings made by scraping the side of the knife blade down each ear (4½ to 5 cups)

¾ cup crushed Carr's Croissant Crackers, oyster crackers, or saltine crackers

3 tablespoons unsalted butter, melted

2 to 3 ounces sharp cheddar, grated (½ to ¾ cup)

Sweet paprika

HIGH SUMMER BLOCK PARTY

Pineapple, Soy, and Pepper Skirt Steak (page 52)

Corn Pudding

BLT Salad with Warm Bacon Dressing (page 158)

Sliced peaches and cream

Preheat the oven to 350°F. Grease a medium baking dish.

Whisk the eggs and half-and-half together in a large bowl with the salt, white pepper, and nutmeg. Mix in the corn kernels and scrapings, ½ cup of the cracker crumbs, and 2 tablespoons of the melted butter. Spoon the pudding into the prepared baking dish and scatter the cheese over it. In a small bowl, mix together the remaining crackers and butter, and sprinkle them over the cheese. Dust with paprika for a bit of extra color.

Bake the pudding for 45 to 50 minutes, until puffed and golden brown. The edges should be a bit crusty, but the center still a little soft. Serve the pudding hot.

PAN DE TOMATE

Thick slabs of garlic bread, toasted on the grill, always taste good, but here's a way to update that basic idea with some Spanish flair. The tomato flavor gets a boost from grill- or oven-dried tomatoes, which will keep for several days. If that part of the process sounds like more work than you want to do, buy a jar of sun-dried tomatoes in oil and use them instead.

Makes 1 dozen large slices

8 red-ripe plum tomatoes
¼ cup flavorful olive oil
½ teaspoon dried thyme, basil, oregano, or marjoram, optional
Coarse salt, either kosher or sea salt

Freshly milled pepper
1 baguette, sliced thickly on the diagonal into 12 pieces
2 plump garlic cloves, halved

Preheat the oven or a covered grill to 250°F. Arrange a piece of parchment on a baking sheet.

Cut 6 of the tomatoes lengthwise into 4 slices each. Toss the tomatoes together in a shallow bowl with 2 tablespoons of the oil and the optional herbs.

Lay the tomato slices on the baking sheet and season generously with salt and pepper. Bake in the oven or covered grill for about 2½ hours, until the slices are somewhat dry and shriveled but still soft and glistening. (The tomatoes can be cooled, covered, and refrigerated for up to several days. Bring back to room temperature before using.)

Fire up the grill, bringing the heat to medium-low (6 to 7 seconds with the hand test). Toast the bread briefly on both sides, until lightly colored and crisp. Smear the toast pieces on one side with the cut side of a garlic clove, pressing it firmly. As each garlic half gets used up, move on to the others. Brush each toast lightly with the remaining oil. Slice the two remaining tomatoes in half lengthwise and firmly smear the cut sides over the bread slices. When done, you shouldn't have much left other than the raggedy tomato skins to discard. Top each slice of toast with a couple of the dried tomatoes and serve.

MELON WITH SPARKLING WINE

During much of the summer and into the fall, few simple desserts beat a cool fragrant slice of melon. While it needs no enhancement, melon welcomes an occasional special touch, such as a little honey and sparkling wine.

Serves 4 or more

1 tablespoon mild-flavored honey

½ large honeydew melon or other green-fleshed melon, cut in bite-size chunks

½ large cantaloupe, casaba, or Crenshaw melon, or other orange- or yellow-fleshed melon, cut in bite-size chunks

1 split (small 187-ml bottle) sparkling wine

Boil the honey and ⅓ cup water together in a small saucepan until the honey is dissolved. Cool.

Spoon the honey syrup over the melon chunks. Divide the melon between glasses, goblets, or bowls, refrigerating briefly until serving time. Pour sparkling wine equally over each portion. Serve immediately.

GINGER BLONDIES

Brownies make wonderful grill party desserts, but everybody has a brownie recipe or three. These ginger-laced blondies satisfy the same craving for something gloriously homey and gooey.

Makes one 7 × 11-inch or
9 × 13-inch pan, about 24 blondies

Butter for the pan
2 cups unbleached all-purpose flour
1 tablespoon ground ginger
1½ teaspoons ground cinnamon
1 teaspoon baking powder
¼ teaspoon ground nutmeg
¾ cup plus 2 tablespoons unsalted butter, softened

1¼ cups granulated sugar
3 tablespoons molasses
2 tablespoons light corn syrup
2 large eggs
¼ cup chopped crystallized ginger
Confectioners' sugar

Preheat the oven to 350°F. Butter a 7 by 11-inch pan. We've also made these in the more common 9 by 13-inch pan, and if that's what you have, use it. The blondies will be thinner but still nicely gooey.

Stir together the flour, ginger, cinnamon, baking powder, and nutmeg.

With an electric mixer on high speed, beat together the butter and sugar for several minutes until light and fluffy, then add the molasses and corn syrup and continue beating on medium speed until well incorporated. Mix in the eggs one at a time, beating until each is blended. On low speed, add about one half of the flour mixture, then add the rest as the first flour disappears into the mixture. Beat just until the flour is blended, stopping if needed to scrape down the sides of the bowl. Stir in the crystallized ginger by hand.

Spread the batter (which will be thick) in the prepared pan, smoothing the surface. Bake for 25 to 30 minutes (22 to 25 minutes for a 9 by 13-inch pan), until the top looks lightly set and a toothpick inserted into the center comes out almost but not quite clean. Avoid overcooking the blondies—when they look completely done, they'll be too dry. Cool the blondies in the pan. Cut to your preferred size. We make squares of about 2 inches and then bisect them into triangles. Slicing is easiest if you wipe the knife blade after each cut. Shortly before serving, dust the blondies with confectioners' sugar, sprinkled through a fine sieve.

BERRY RIGHT-SIDE-UP CAKE

This pretty baked dessert is one part cake, one part tart, and altogether scrumptious.

Serves 8 to 10

Butter for the pan

1 cup plus 2 tablespoons unbleached all-purpose flour

1 teaspoon baking powder

½ teaspoon table salt

1 cup slivered almonds

½ cup (1 stick) butter, in several chunks, softened

¾ cup sugar

3 large eggs, at room temperature

1 teaspoon pure vanilla extract

¼ teaspoon almond extract

1 cup crème fraîche, at room temperature

2 heaping cups raspberries, blueberries, blackberries, or a combination

Confectioners' sugar

Preheat the oven to 375°F. Butter a 10-inch springform pan.

Whisk together the flour, baking powder, and salt in a food processor. Add the almonds and pulse to process until the mixture resembles a fine meal. Dump the mixture into a medium bowl.

Without rinsing out the processor, cream the butter and sugar together in it until light and fluffy, about 20 seconds. Add the eggs one at a time, incorporating each fully with a few pulses. Follow with the vanilla and almond extracts. Pour about one half of the flour mixture back into the processor and pulse to combine, then add and pulse in the rest of the flour mixture. Scrape the batter into the prepared pan. The layer of batter will look rather thin. Drop the crème fraîche over the batter in tablespoon-size dollops, covering it more or less evenly but not thoroughly. Top with the berries. Bake for 30 to 35 minutes until the surface is golden brown and a toothpick inserted in the center comes out clean.

Remove to a baking rack. Cool for 10 minutes, then run a knife around the inside edge of the pan to loosen the cake and remove the springform. Cool at least 5 more minutes, then slice and serve. Dust with confectioners' sugar just before serving, if you are using it.

PIÑA COLADA SORBET

We love icy piña coladas, but always think they should be a dessert. Now they are.

1 quart pineapple or tropical fruit sorbet, or 1 pint pineapple or tropical fruit sorbet and 1 pint coconut sorbet

One 8-ounce can crushed pineapple, drained

One 8-ounce can cream of coconut (not coconut milk)

¼ cup white rum

2 tablespoons fresh lime juice

Let the sorbet sit at room temperature until softened, about 45 minutes. If you're in a hurry, give it a few brief zaps in the microwave. Pour into a bowl. Add the remaining ingredients and whisk together. Freeze until set, generally a couple of hours, stirring a couple of times and redistributing the pineapple pieces. (To speed it along, freeze it in a broad, shallow dish.) It will remain a bit chunky. The sorbet is best the day it's made, but will keep up to a week.

Adding a Personal Signature:

Enhance the sorbet by serving it with some grilled spears of fresh pineapple. Brush them with butter and cook on a medium fire for about 5 to 6 minutes. If the party's for grown-ups, pass dark rum to pour over scoops of the sorbet.

ICE CREAM SUNDAE DESSERT BAR

Create a backyard ice cream social with this action-plan recipe. Add or subtract items for the sundae bar depending on the size of the meal, the number of kids and other guests, and how much freezer space you can devote to ice cream and related frozen treats. Then invite everyone to create their own ice cream sculpture.

Serves as many as you wish

Several varieties of ice cream, sorbet, sherbet, and/or gelato

Berries, sliced fresh fruit, and/or grilled fruit from the previous chapter (pages 149 to 154)

Several varieties of dessert sauces and/or syrups

Fresh or candied citrus peel

Almonds, hazelnuts, pecans, walnuts, peanuts, and/or other nuts

Chocolate-covered coffee beans, chocolate shavings from a candy bar, and/or espresso and cocoa powders

Softly whipped cream

For adults, a few alcoholic options such as dark or spiced rum, schnapps, tequila, bourbon, or dessert wine to use as a topping

A few silly touches like mini-marshmallows, candy confetti, crushed peppermints, chopped cookies or candy bars, and/or stoplight-bright maraschino cherries

Pick out the shadiest spot in your yard for the sundae bar. Pack the ice creams into one or more big bowls or a tub of ice and surround them with dishes of berries and fruit. Set out everything else with spoons and bowls nearby. You won't need to encourage digging in.

Adding a Personal Signature:

Instead of offering a bar full of choices, serve one or two of special sundaes that appeal to you. Some of our favorites include:

lime and orange sorbets with lime and orange zests and tequila; grilled peaches over butter pecan ice cream with a bourbon splash; vanilla ice cream with strawberries, crushed peppermints, and strawberry sauce; coconut ice cream or gelato with chopped Mounds candy bars, chocolate-covered coffee beans, and bittersweet chocolate syrup.

MOCHA BROWNIE ICE CREAM CAKE

When you want to say "I made it myself," here's a casual party treat that will win you raves. The ice cream-topped fudgy brownie "cake" can be prepared a day or two ahead. The cake is especially good with the suggested Ben & Jerry's ice cream, but many other kinds work great as well.

Serves 8 to 12

BROWNIE CAKE

Butter for the pan

½ pound good quality bittersweet chocolate, chopped

¾ cup (1½ sticks) unsalted butter, in several chunks

2 teaspoons pure vanilla extract

1 tablespoon instant espresso powder dissolved in 1 tablespoon boiling water

1½ cups sugar

½ teaspoon table salt

4 large eggs

1 cup unbleached all-purpose flour

1 pint Ben & Jerry's Coffee HEATH Bar Crunch ice cream, or other compatibly flavored ice cream, such as coffee, vanilla, milk chocolate, butter pecan, or peanut butter

GLAZE

½ pound good quality bittersweet chocolate, chopped

2 tablespoons unsalted butter

½ cup heavy whipping cream

1 tablespoon instant espresso powder dissolved in 1 tablespoon boiling water

Preheat the oven to 350°F. Butter a 10-inch springform pan.

Prepare the brownie layer. Melt together the chocolate and butter in a small saucepan, stirring over very low heat. Remove from the heat while a few lumps remain. Continue to stir, finishing the melting with the residual heat of the pan. Scrape the mixture into a medium bowl and let it cool for about 5 minutes. By hand, stir in the vanilla, espresso mixture, sugar, and salt, and then the eggs one at a time. Stir in the flour, mixing only just until combined. Spoon the batter into the prepared pan. Bake for 25 to 30 minutes, until the top looks just set and a toothpick inserted in the center comes out almost but not quite clean. Cool to room temperature.

While the brownies cool, let the ice cream sit out at room temperature.

Prepare the glaze. Melt together the chocolate and butter with the cream and espresso mixture, stirring until the glaze is smooth. Set the glaze aside to cool.

Pack the softened ice cream over the brownie layer, smoothing the top. Place in the freezer for about 30 minutes or until the ice cream is firm. Spread the glaze over the ice cream and return to the freezer for at least 1 more hour, preferably two. If you want to hold the ice cream cake for another day, cover with plastic wrap. Before serving, let it sit in the refrigerator briefly, then run a knife around the inside of the springform pan and unmold. Slice into wedges with a sharp knife, wiped off after each cut. Promptly return any leftovers to the freezer.

SANGRIA BLANCA

If something goes wrong at a party, keep a sense of humor about it and it may end up being the thing people remember most fondly. All the guests had a huge laugh the time that Cheryl mistakenly used Bill's premier cognac instead of inexpensive brandy in a batch of sangria. Not only did they polish off the pitcher in record time, they're still talking about it. If you avoid that mistake, sangria goes a long way on a small budget and isn't likely to cause too much giddiness.

Makes about 2 quarts

⅔ cup sugar

1 cup mango juice, orange-mango juice, pineapple-orange juice, or other compatible fruit juice or juice blend, or more to taste

½ cup fresh lime juice

1 medium orange or large tangerine, sliced in thin rounds

1 large lime or medium lemon, sliced in thin rounds

A handful seedless grapes, halved

¼ cup Triple Sec or other orange liqueur, or more to taste

¼ cup inexpensive brandy or fruit brandy, such as peach

4 cups inexpensive dry white wine, chilled

1 to 2 cups sparkling water or club soda, chilled

A handful raspberries or sliced strawberries, optional

Combine the sugar, fruit juices, fruit slices, and grapes in a pitcher, and stir until the sugar dissolves. Let the mixture stand for 15 to 30 minutes. Pour in the liqueurs, wine, and sparkling water to taste (remembering that you'll add ice before serving, which will water down the sangria more). Chill if not serving immediately. Serve over ice in goblets or other glasses, with a bit of the fruit added to each portion. Add a few berries at the end for color, if you wish.

CHAMPAGNE COOLERS

A bottle of bubbly makes the most casual of get-togethers feel special. Start with an inexpensive sparkling wine—such as Italian Prosecco, Spanish cava, or our favorite, American-made Gruet—and just add a touch of fruit and mint.

Serves up to 8

Peach or mango liqueur, or both
Store-bought mint syrup (the type used in coffee and other beverages), preferably uncolored

1 bottle sparkling white wine, well-chilled
Fresh mint sprigs

Pour about 1 inch of fruit liqueur into the bottoms of champagne flutes. Add a teaspoon-size splash of mint syrup to each. Fill with sparkling wine, garnish with mint sprigs, and serve.

CARIBBEAN RUM PUNCH

When people welcome you in the islands, a rum punch invariably follows a handshake. These are best made by the glass, which allows you to show off your bartending skills, however rusty they may be. Just get yourself a jigger and pour away.

Makes 1 potent punch

2 ounces white or gold rum

1 ounce spiced rum such as Captain Morgan's, or vanilla rum

2 ounces pineapple or orange juice, or a combination

½ ounce (1 tablespoon) fresh lime juice

½ ounce (1 tablespoon) simple syrup

1 teaspoon grenadine syrup

2 drops Angostura bitters

Nutmeg

Orange slice, lime slice, maraschino cherry, or a combination

In a tall glass combine the two rums, fruit juices, simple syrup, grenadine syrup, and bitters. Stir well and add ice to the top of the glass. Grate or sprinkle nutmeg over the top. Garnish with an orange slice on the rim and serve.

CHIMAYÓ COCKTAILS BY THE PITCHER

The Restaurante Rancho de Chimayó, in the small New Mexico village of Chimayó, developed the original version of this tequila-and-apple elixir that we have adopted as our own house cocktail. A satisfying drink summer or winter, it's easily made with ingredients you can keep on hand to mix up whenever company calls.

Serves up to 8

2 cups (16 ounces) apple cider or unsweetened apple juice

1 cup (8 ounces) tequila, preferably gold

¼ cup (2 ounces) crème de cassis

¼ cup (2 ounces) fresh lemon juice

Ice cubes

Unpeeled apple slices, optional

In a pitcher, stir together the cider, tequila, crème de cassis, and lemon juice. Half-fill 8-ounce glasses with ice. Pour the drink into the glasses, garnish each with an apple slice, if you like, and serve.

TGIF COCKTAIL PARTY

Chimayó Cocktails by the Pitcher

Caribbean Rum Punch (page 178)

Goat Cheese Wrapped in Grape Leaves (page 15)

Sausages and Baby Onions with Three Mustards (page 20)

Spicy green olives